POCKET
POSITIVES

More
POCKET POSITIVES

Compiled by Maggie Pinkney

The Five Mile Press

The Five Mile Press

The Five Mile Press Pty Ltd
22 Summit Road
Noble Park Victoria 3174
Australia

Published in 1999
Reprinted 2000, 2002

Editor: Maggie Pinkney
Cover design: Sonia Juraja
Formatting: Louise Taylor

Printed in Australia by Griffin Press

National Library of Australia
Cataloguing-in-publication data

Includes index.
ISBN 1 86503 165 8

1. Quotations, English. 2. Optimism-Quotations, maxims, etc. 3.
Success-Quotations, maxims, etc.
082

COVER PHOTOGRAPH
White Clouds
Stock Photos Pty Ltd

Contents

Introduction	7
Ability – Authority	9
Balance – Boredom	36
Challenges – Curiosity	49
Death – Dreams	85
Education – Experience	93
Failure – Friendship	111
Gardens & Gardening – Guilt	138
Habit – Humour	160
Ideals & Idealism – Invention	181
Joy – Justice	193
Kindness – Knowledge	197
Laughter – Luck	201
Marriage – Music	220
Nature	229
Obstacles – Originality	233
Parting – Problems	241
Regret – Risk	257
Self-acceptance – Sympathy	267
Tact – Truth	290
Understanding – Unity	301
Victory – Vocation	302
Walking – Worth	305
Yesterday, Today & Tomorrow – Youth	319
Zeal	326
Subject Index	327
Index of Sources	330

Introduction

Mankind would lose half its wisdom built up over centuries if it lost its great sayings. They contain the best parts of the best books.

Thomas Jefferson (1743-1826)

The resounding success of *Pocket Positives* has inspired us to assemble this new anthology of benign and healing thoughts to provide you with encouragement and inspiration. Again, these quotations are drawn from a wide range of sources — including the world's greatest philosophers, religious leaders, poets, novelists and humorists, as well as people from many other walks of life.

What all these men and women — from the distant past to the present — have in common is the ability to inspire us in some way, whether it is with their love, enthusiasm, compassion, courage, wisdom, success or pure zest for life. It's not that they are superhuman. Many quotations reveal that their authors are deeply acquainted with sorrows, failures and fears. But they have managed to keep sight of the larger picture, and to fight back. In fact, one of the most comforting aspects of this anthology is that it shows us that whatever our problems are, we are not alone. Someone else, somewhere, has felt as we do, and has experienced what we are going through. This is in itself a consolation, and certainly helps one to gain an all-important sense of perspective.

In this selection, many themes occur again and again — each time expressed in a fresh new way. For example, Austrian psychiatrist Alfred Adler wrote, 'We can be cured of depression in only fourteen days if every day we will try to think of how we can be helpful to others.' Mark Twain reached the same conclusion: 'The best way to cheer yourself up is to cheer someone else up,' he advised. A similar sentiment is expressed yet again — and with great elegance — by Ralph Waldo Emerson: 'It is one of the most beautiful compensations of this life that no man can sincerely try to help another without helping himself.'

Some of the famous men and women who share their thoughts with us in these 'pocket positives' give us a sense of understanding and acceptance. Others, such as Martin Luther King, Winston Churchill, Aung San Suu Kyi and Helen Keller, inspire us by their example as much as by their words.

Quotations are arranged under subject heads for easy reference, and an index of sources is also included. Keep this companionable anthology by your bedside and read it regularly. It will help you to enjoy a more fulfilling and meaningful life. Simply open it at any page until you find a quote that 'speaks' to you in your present frame of mind. As Albert Einstein said, 'There are two ways to live your life. One is as though nothing is a miracle. The other is as though everything is a miracle.'

Welcome to *More Pocket Positives*!

A

Ability

One of the greatest of all principles is that men can do what they think they can do.

Norman Vincent Peale, 1898-1993
American writer and minister

It is better to have a little ability and use it well than to have much ability and make poor use of it.

Anonymous

They are able who think they are able.

Virgil, 70-19 BC
Roman poet

Achievement

It was a golden year beyond my dreams. I proved you're never too old to achieve what you really want to do.

Heather Turland, b. 1960
Australian women's marathon gold medallist,
Commonwealth Games, 1998

Achievement is largely the product of steadily raising one's level of aspiration and expectation.

Jack Nicklaus, b. 1940
American golfer

All the things we achieve are things we have first of all imagined and then made happen.

David Malouf, b. 1934
Australian writer

Action

To will is to select a goal, determine a course
of action that will bring one to that goal, and
then hold to that action till the goal is reached.
The key is action.

Michael Hanson, 1863-1908
American mathematician

Action is the antidote to despair.

Joan Baez, b. 1941
American folk singer

Well done is better than well said.

Benjamin Franklin, 1706-1790
American statesman and scientist

A little knowledge that *acts* is worth infinitely
more than knowledge that is idle.

Kahlil Gibran, 1882-1931
Lebanese poet, artist and mystic

In our era the road to holiness necessarily passes through the world of action.

Dag Hammarskjold, 1905-1961
Swedish statesman and humanitarian

Just go out there and do what you've got to do.

Martina Navratilova, b. 1956
Czechoslovakian-born American tennis champion

Don't wait for a light to appear at the end of the tunnel, stride down there . . . and light the bloody thing yourself.

Sara Henderson, b. 1936
Australian outback station manager and writer

As life is action and passion, it is required of man that he should share the passion and action of his time, at peril of being judged not to have lived.

Oliver Wendell Holmes, 1809-1894
American writer and physician

All mankind is divided into three classes: those that are immovable, those that are movable, and those that move.

Benjamin Franklin, 1706-1790
American statesman and scientist

The shortest answer is doing.

English proverb

A good deed, no matter how small, is worth more than all the good intentions in the world.

Anonymous

You can't build a reputation on what you're going to do.

Henry Ford, 1863-1946
American car manufacturer

Knowledge without Action is useless. Action without Knowledge is foolishness.

Sai Baba
Indian spiritual master

However brilliant an action may be it should not be esteemed great unless the result of a great motive.

Duc de La Rochefoucauld 1613-1680
French writer

Action may not always bring happiness, but there is no happiness without action.

Benjamin Disraeli, 1804-1881
British Prime Minister and writer

How may a man gain self-knowledge? By contemplation? Certainly not; but by action. Try to do your duty and you will find what you are fit for. But what is your duty? The demand of the hour.

Johann von Goethe, 1749-1832
German writer, dramatist and scientist

Our grand business in life is not to see what lies dimly at a distance, but to do what clearly lies at hand.

Thomas Carlyle, 1795-1881
Scottish historian, essayist and critic

Sometimes the only way for me to find out what it is I want to do is go ahead and do something. Then the moment I start to act, my feelings become clear.

Hugh Prather, b. 1938
American writer

The man who does things makes many mistakes, but he never makes the biggest mistake of all — doing nothing.

Benjamin Franklin, 1706-1790
American statesman and scientist

Adventurousness

Not all those that wander are lost.

J. R. R. Tolkien, 1892-1973
English author

Adversity

A man of character finds a special
attractiveness in difficulty, since it is only by
coming to grips with difficulty that he can
realise his potentialities.

Charles de Gaulle, 1890-1970
French statesman and general

A woman is like a teabag — you can't tell how
strong she is until you put her in hot water.

Nancy Reagan, b. 1923
First Lady of the United States of America

Adversity introduces a man to himself.

Anonymous

When you're up to your ears in trouble, try
using the part that isn't submerged.

Anonymous

Advice

If I were asked to give what I consider the single most useful piece of advice for all humanity it would be this: Expect trouble as an inevitable part of life, and when it comes, hold your head high, look it squarely in the eye and say, 'I will be bigger than you. You cannot defeat me.' Then repeat to yourself the most comforting words of all, 'This too will pass.'

Ann Landers, b. 1918
American advice columnist

Seek ye counsel of the aged, for their eyes have looked on the faces of the years and their ears have hearkened to the voices of Life. Even if their counsel is displeasing to you, pay heed to them.

Kahlil Gibran, 1883-1931
Lebanese poet, artist and mystic

When you can, always advise people to
do what you see they really want to do, so
long as what they want to do isn't dangerously
unlawful, stupidly unsocial or obviously
imposssible. Doing what they want to do,
they may succeed; doing what they don't
want to do, they won't.

James Gould Cozzens, 1903-1978
American writer

Do a little more than you're paid to;
Give a little more than you have to;
Try a little harder than you want to;
Aim a little higher than you think possible;
And give a lot of thanks to God for health,
family and friends.

Art Linkletter
American television personality

Consult your friend on all things, especially on
those which concern yourself. His counsel may
then be useful where your own self-love may
impair your judgement.

Seneca, c. 4 BC - 65 AD
Roman philosopher, dramatist, poet and statesman

Whenever you are asked if you can do a job, tell 'em, 'Certainly I can!' — and get busy and find out how to do it.

Theodore Roosevelt, 1858-1919
President of the United States of America

We have to steer our true life's course. Whatever your calling is in life! The whole purpose of being here is to figure out what that is as soon as possible, so you go about the business of being on track, of not being owned by what your mother said, what society said, whatever people think a woman is supposed to be . . . when you can exceed other people's expectations and be defined by your own!

Oprah Winfrey, b. 1954
American television personality

Generosity gives assistance rather than advice.

Marquis de Vauvenargues, 1715-1745
French soldier and writer

Ageing

Old age is not an illness, it is a timeless
ascent. As power diminishes, we grow
toward the light.

May Sarton, 1912-1995
American writer and poet

One should never count the years — one
should count one's interests. I have kept young
trying never to lose my childhood sense of
wonderment. I am glad I still have a vivid
curiosity about the world I live in.

Helen Keller, 1880-1968
Blind and deaf American writer and scholar

Wrinkles should merely indicate where smiles
have been.

Mark Twain, 1835-1910
American humorist and writer

Ageing is a life-spanning process of growth and development from birth to death. Old age is an integral part of the whole, bringing fulfilment and self-actualisation. I regard ageing as a triumph, a result of strength and survivorship.

Margaret Kuhn, b. 1905
American civil rights activist

I have no romantic feelings about age. Either you are interesting at any age or you are not. There is nothing particularly interesting about being old — or being young, for that matter.

Katharine Hepburn, b. 1907
American actress

There is nothing more liberating than age.

Liz Carpenter, b. 1920
American feminist writer

I am delighted to be with you. In fact, at my age, I am delighted to be anywhere.

Ronald Reagan, b. 1911
President of the United States of America

Thank God I have the seeing eye, that is to say, as I lie in bed I can walk step by step on the fells and rough land seeing every stone and flower and patch of bog and cotton pass where my old legs will never take me again.

Beatrix Potter, 1866-1943
British children's writer and illustrator

The wiser mind
Mourns less for what age takes away
Than what it leaves behind.

William Wordsworth, 1770-1850
English poet

It is quite wrong to think of old age as a down-ward slope. On the contrary, one climbs higher and higher with the advancing years, and that, too, with surprising strides. Brain-work comes as easily to the old as physical exertion to the child. One is moving, it is true, towards the end of life, but that end is now a goal, and not a reef in which the vessel may be dashed.

George Sand (Amandine Dupin) 1804-1876
French novelist

By the bye, as I must leave off being young, I find many Douceurs in being a sort of Chaperone for I am put on the Sofa near the fire and can drink as much wine as I like.

Jane Austen, 1775-1816
English novelist
From a letter to her sister Cassandra

I prefer to forget both pairs of glasses and spend my declining years saluting strange women and grandfather clocks.

Ogden Nash, 1902-1971
American humorous poet

Perhaps middle age is, or should be, a period of shedding shells: the shell of ambition, the shell of material accumulations and possessions, the shell of ego.

Anne Morrow Lindbergh, b. 1906
American writer

I am still not ready to accept completely grey hair. I try to keep fit — eat vegetarian meals, walk, swim and practise yoga. Mostly I accept my body as a record of my life.

Margaret Henry, b. 1934
Australian writer

I am 65 and I guess that puts me in with the geriatrics. But if there were 15 months in every year, I'd only be 48. That's the trouble with us. We number everything. Take women, for example, I think they deserve to have more than 12 years between the ages of 28 and 40.

James Thurber, 1894-1961
American writer and cartoonist

Our hearts are young 'neath wrinkled rind: life's more interesting than we thought.

Andrew Lang, 1844-1912
Scottish poet

When I passed the seventieth milestone ten months ago I instantly realised that I had entered a new country and a new atmosphere... I now believe that the best of life begins at seventy, for then your work is done; you know that you have done your best, let the quality of the work be what it may; that you have earned your holiday...and that henceforth to the setting of the sun nothing will break it, nothing interrupt it.

Mark Twain, 1835-1910
American humorist and writer

I gave my youth and beauty to men. I am going to give my wisdom and experience to animals.

Brigitte Bardot, b. 1934
French actress and animal rights campaigner

One of the signs of passing youth is the birth of a sense of fellowship with other human beings as we take our place among them.

Virginia Woolf, 1882-1941
English novelist

Becoming a grandmother is more often
a middle-age than an old-age event. For
many women today this is a time when, free
of immediate family responsibilities, they
discover new skills and at last are able to do
what they want to do. The idea of old age is
also changing. Women in their sixties and
seventies do not get old. Instead we enter an
active and satisfying 'third age', and after that,
at eighty, a happy and contented 'fourth age'.

Sheila Kitzinger, b. 1929
Obstetrician and writer

Life has got to be lived — that's all there
is to it. At seventy, I would say the advantage
is that you take life more calmly. You know
that 'this too will pass!'

Eleanor Roosevelt, 1884-1962
*First Lady of the United States of America, writer and
diplomat*

Grow old along with me!
The best is yet to be.

Robert Browning, 1812-1889
English poet

The process of maturing is an art to be learned, an effort to be sustained. By the age of fifty you have made yourself what you are and, if it is good, it is better than your youth.

Marya Mannes, b. 1904
American journalist

Age puzzles me. I thought it was a quiet time. My seventies were interesting and fairly serene, but my eighties are passionate. I grow more intense as I age.

Florida Scott-Maxwell, 1833-1979
American-born English writer and psychologist

Age only matters when one is ageing. Now that I have arrived at a great age, I might as well be twenty.

Pablo Picasso, 1881-1973
Spanish painter and sculptor

Ambition

Ambition never gets anywhere until it forms a
partnership with work.

Anonymous

If you wish in this world to advance
Your merits you're bound to enhance,
You must stir it and stump it,
And blow your own trumpet
Or, trust me, you haven't a chance!

W. S. Gilbert, 1836-1911
English dramatist and librettist

The fellow who has an abundance of push gets
along very well without pull.

Anonymous

Anger

Anybody can become angry. That is not difficult; but to be angry with the right person and to the right degree, and at the right time, and for the right purpose, and in the right way: that is not within everybody's capability and it is not easy.

Aristotle, 384-322 BC
Greek philosopher

For every minute you remain angry you give up sixty seconds of peace of mind.

Ralph Waldo Emerson, 1803-1882
American essayist, poet and philosopher

Anger is short-lived in a good man.

Thomas Fuller, 1608-1661
English clergyman and writer

Animals

Love the animals: God has given them the
rudiments of thought and joy untroubled.

Feodor Dostoevsky, 1821-1881
Russian writer

All animals except man know that the
ultimate of life is to enjoy it.

Samuel Butler, 1835-1902
English writer

God made all the animals and gave
them our love and our fear,
To give sign, we and they are his children,
one family here.

Robert Browning, 1812-1889
English poet

Heaven goes by favour. If it went by merit, you
would stay out and your dog would go in.

Mark Twain, 1835-1910
American humorist and writer

I think I could turn and live with animals,
they're so placid and self-contained. I stand
and look at them long and long.

Walt Whitman, 1819-1892
American poet and writer

Our perfect companions never have
fewer than four feet.

Colette, 1873-1954
French writer

I really don't think I could consent to
go to Heaven if I thought there were to
be no animals there.

George Bernard Shaw, 1856-1950
Irish writer, dramatist and critic

Apology

A man should never be ashamed to own
he has been in the wrong, which is but saying,
in other words, that he is wiser today
than he was yesterday.

Alexander Pope, 1688-1744
English poet

A true apology is more than just
acknowledgement of a mistake. It is
recognition that something you have said or
done has damaged a relationship and that you
care enough about the relationship to want it
repaired and restored.

Norman Vincent Peale, 1898-1993
American writer and minister

A sincere apology takes courage and humility.

Anonymous

Attitude

I've never been poor, only broke. Being poor
is a frame of mind. Being broke is only
a temporary setback.

Mike Todd, 1903-1958
American film producer

The greater part of our happiness or
misery depends on our dispositions and
not our circumstances.

Martha Washington, 1732-1802
First Lady of the United States of America

There is nothing either good or bad, but
thinking makes it so.

William Shakespeare, 1564-1616
English poet and playwright

I don't sing because I'm happy;
I'm happy because I sing.

William James, 1842-1910
American psychologist and philosopher

If, from time to time, we look at the blessings
in our lives, at the warmth and care and love
so many people respond with when there is a
tragedy, at the fact that we can walk and talk,
eat and breathe, then maybe we would re-
evaluate our bad moods and become aware
that all negative thoughts bring with them
more negativity, but all love shared
returns a thousandfold.
'As a man thinketh' perhaps best describes how
we are the creators of our own worlds.

Elisabeth Kübler-Ross, b. 1926
Swiss-born American psychiatrist

I always prefer to believe the best of
everybody; it saves so much trouble.

Rudyard Kipling, 1865-1936
Indian-born British poet and writer

Life appears to me too short to be spent in nursing animosity or registering wrong.

Charlotte Brontë, 1816-1855
British novelist

It is our attitude at the beginning of a difficult undertaking which, more than anything else, will determine its successful outcome.

William James, 1842-1910
American psychologist and philosopher

Nothing can hurt you unless you give it the power to do so.

A Course in Miracles

Authority

When you make peace with authority, you become authority.

Jim Morrison, 1943-1971
American rock singer

B

Balance

There are as many nights as days, and the one is just as long as the other in the year's course. Even a happy life cannot be without a measure of darkness, and the word 'happy' would lose its meaning if it were not balanced by sadness. It is far better to take things as they come along with patience and equanimity.

Carl Jung, 1875-1961
Swiss psychiatrist

Everyone is a moon and has a dark side which he never shows to anybody.

Mark Twain, 1835-1910
American humorist and writer

To be a woman is to have interests and duties, raying out in all directions from the central mother-core, like spokes from the hub of a wheel . . . We must be open to all points of the compass; husband, children, friends, home, community; stretched out, exposed, like a spider's web to each breeze that blows, to each call that comes. How difficult for us, then, to achieve a balance in the midst of these contradictory tensions, and yet how necessary for the proper functioning of our lives.

Anne Morrow Lindbergh, b. 1906
American writer

Beauty

Beauty is the gift of God.

Aristotle, 384-322 BC
Greek philosopher

Cheerfulness and contentment are great beautifiers and are famous preservers of youthful good looks.

Charles Dickens, 1812-1870
English writer

Everything has its beauty but not
everyone sees it.

Confucius, c. 550-c. 478 BC
Chinese philosopher

Beauty is God's handwriting,
Welcome it
in every fair face,
every fair day,
every fair flower.

Charles Kingsley, 1819-1875
English writer, poet and clergyman

Beauty is no quality in things themselves;
it exists merely in the mind which
contemplates them; and each mind
perceives a different beauty.

David Hume, 1711-1776
Scottish philosopher and historian

Beginning

The distance doesn't matter; it is only
the first step that is difficult.

Marquise de Deffand, 1697-1780
French noblewoman

There is an old saying 'well begun is half done'
. . . I would use instead — Not begun at
all until half done.

John Keats, 1795-1821
English poet

The right moment for starting on your next job
is not tomorrow or next week; it is *instanter*,
or in the American idiom, right now.

Arnold Toynbee, 1899-1975
English historian

Belief

Believe you can, and you can. Belief is one of the most powerful of all problem dissolvers. When you believe that a difficulty can be overcome, you are more than halfway to victory over it already.

Norman Vincent Peale, 1898-1993
American writer and minister

I believe in one God and no more, and I hope for happiness beyond this life. I believe in the equality of man; and I believe that religious duties consist in doing justice, loving mercy and in endeavouring to make our fellow creatures happy.

Thomas Paine, 1737-1809
English-born American revolutionary philosopher and writer

No one of you is a believer until he desires for his brother that which he desires for himself.

Islamic spirituality

Best

I do the very best I know how — the very best I can; and I mean to keep on doing it until the end.

Abraham Lincoln, 1809-1865
American statesman and President

When we do the best we can, we never know what miracle is wrought in our life, or the life of another.

Helen Keller, 1880-1968
Blind and deaf American writer and scholar

I have tried simply to write the best I can; sometimes I have good luck and write better than I can.

Ernest Hemingway, 1898-1961
American writer

Blessings

Let there be many windows in your soul,
That all the glories of the universe
May beautify it.

Ralph Waldo Trine, 1866-1958
American poet and writer

Bless the four corners of this little house
And be the lintel blessed;
And bless the hearth, and bless the board
And bless each place of rest.

Anonymous

Reflect on your present blessings, of
which every man has many, not on your past
misfortunes, of which all men have some.

Charles Dickens, 1812-1870
English writer

Books

No entertainment is so cheap as reading,
nor any pleasure so lasting.

Lady Mary Wortley Montague, 1689-1762
English poet and writer

Then I thought of reading — the nice and
subtle happiness of reading . . . this joy not
dulled by age, this polite and unpunishable
vice, this selfish, serene, lifelong intoxication.

Logan Pearsall Smith, 1865-1946
American essayist

A good book is the precious lifeblood of a
master spirit, embalmed and treasured up on
purpose to a life beyond life.

John Milton, 1608-1674
English poet

A library is thought in cold storage.

Herbert Samuel, 1870-1963
British statesman

For books are more than books,
they are the life
The very heart and core of ages past,
The reason why men lived and
worked and died,
The essence and quintessence of their lives.

Amy Lowell, 1874-1925
American poet and writer

Study has been for me the sovereign remedy
against all the disappointments of life. I have
never known any trouble that an hour's
reading would not dissipate.

Charles Louis de Montesquieu, 1689-1755
French political philosopher

Books are the legacies that a great genius leaves
to mankind, which are delivered down from
generation to generation as presents to the
posterity of those who are not yet born.

Joseph Addison, 1672-1719
English essayist

The books read in childhood . . . create in one's mind a sort of false map of the world, a series of fabulous countries into which one can retreat at odd moments throughout the rest of life, and which in some cases can even survive a visit to the real countries which they are supposed to represent.

George Orwell, 1903-1950
English novelist and essayist

Books, books, books. It was not that I read so much. I read and re-read the same ones. But all of them were necessary to me. Their presence, their smell, the letters of their titles, and the texture of their leather bindings.

Colette, 1873-1954
French writer

We read books to find out who we are. What other people, real or imaginary, do and think and feel is an essential guide to our understanding of what we ourselves are and may become.

Ursula LeGuin, b. 1929
American science fiction writer

The best effect of any book is that it excites the reader to self activity.

Thomas Carlyle, 1875-1881
Scottish historian, essayist and critic

My early and invincible love of reading I would not exchange for all the riches of India.

Edward Gibbon, 1737-1794
British historian

You may have tangible wealth untold,
Caskets of jewels and coffers of gold.
Richer than I you can never be —
I had a mother who read to me.

Strickland Gillilan, 1869-1954
Writer and poet

Mankind would lose half its wisdom built up over the centuries if it lost its great sayings. They contain the best parts of the best books.

Thomas Jefferson, 1743-1826
President of the United States of America

No furniture so charming as books, even if you never open them, or read a single word.

Sydney Smith, 1771-1845
English clergyman, essayist and wit

. . . books, because of their weight and texture, and because of their sweetly token resistance to manipulation, involve our hands and eyes, and then our minds and souls, in a spiritual adventure I would be very sorry for my grandchildren not to know about.

Kurt Vonnegut, b. 1922
American novelist

When I am attacked by gloomy thoughts, nothing helps me so much as running to my books. They quickly absorb me and banish the clouds from my mind.

Michel de Montaigne, 1533-1592
French essayist

Boredom

Life is so full of exciting things to do and see that we should never be bored. Watch the sunrise from a hot-air balloon, go swimming with dolphins, take up bushwalking, join a book club, learn a foreign language. Try out at least one new and interesting thing each year.

Anonymous

There is no such thing as an uninteresting subject; the only thing that can exist is an uninterested person.

G. K. Chesterton, 1874-1936
English writer and critic

Is not life a hundred times too short for us to bore ourselves?

Friedrich Nietzsche, 1844-1900
German philosopher

C

Challenges

If you continuously face challenges,
one of two things can happen:
You either collapse under the strain, lose
confidence in your ability and walk away
defeated — perhaps to fight again later or to
just drift into a life of non-challenge. Or you
win a few impossibles and are then encouraged
to have a go at the next impossible. So that
before long, you find the impossibles have
become possible.

Sara Henderson, B. 1936
Australian outback station manager and writer

There are no problems — only challenges.

Anonymous

Change

Keep in mind in how many things you yourself
have already seen changes. The universe is
change. Life is understanding.

Marcus Aurelius, 121-180 AD
Roman emperor and philosopher

Life is change. Growth is optional.
Choose wisely.

Karen Kaiser Clark, b. 1938
American legislator and feminist

We must always change, renew, rejuvenate
ourselves; otherwise we harden.

Johann von Goethe, 1749-1832
German writer, dramatist and scientist

Learn to adapt, adjust and accommodate.

Sai Baba
Indian spiritual master

If you don't like the way the world is, you change it. You have an obligation to change it. You just do it one step at a time.

Marian Wright Edelman, b. 1937
American attorney and civil rights activist

The foolish and the dead alone never change their opinions.

James Russell Lowell, 1819-1891
American poet and diplomat

To live is to change, and to be perfect is to have changed often.

Cardinal John Henry Newman, 1801-1890
English theologian and writer

There is no sin punished more implacably by nature than the sin of resistance to change.

Anne Morrow Lindbergh, b. 1906
American writer

Only the wisest and stupidest of men
never change.

Confucius, c. 550-c. 478 BC
Chinese philosopher

If you are not happy with yourself, make a
conscious effort to change whatever it is you
don't like. It is never too late to become a
better, more caring person.

Anonymous

Let us never confuse stability with stagnation.

Mary Jean LeTendre, b. 1948
American educator

Progress is impossible without change; and
those who cannot change their minds cannot
change anything.

George Bernard Shaw, 1856-1950
Irish dramatist, writer and critic

Character

I desire so to conduct the affairs of this
administration that if at the end, when I
come to lay down the reins of power, I have
lost every other friend on earth, I shall at least
have one friend left, and that friend shall
be down inside of me.

Abraham Lincoln, 1809-1865
American statesman and President

The strongest man in the world is the
man who stands alone.

Henrik Ibsen, 1828-1906
Norwegian writer, dramatist and poet

Character-building begins in our infancy
and continues until death.

Eleanor Roosevelt, 1884-1962
*First Lady of the United States of America,
writer and diplomat*

Character cannot be developed in ease and quiet. Only through experience of trial and suffering can the soul be strengthened, vision cleared, ambition inspired and success achieved.

Helen Keller, 1880-1968
Blind and deaf American writer and scholar

The best index to a person's character is how he treats people who can't do him any good, and how he treats people who can't fight back.

Abigail Van Buren, b. 1918
American advice columnist

It is easy in the world to live after the world's opinions. It is easy in solitude to live after our own; but the great man is he who, in the midst of the crowd, keeps with perfect sweetness the independence of solitude.

Ralph Waldo Emerson, 1803-1882
American essayist, poet and philosopher

Children & Parents

Of all the joys that brighten suffering earth,
What joy is welcom'd like a newborn child!

Caroline Norton, 1808-1877
Irish writer and reformer

Every child born into the world is a
new thought of God, an ever fresh and
radiant possibility.

Kate Douglas Wiggin, 1856-1923
American writer and educator

Children are an affirmation of life itself. They
have shown me how much fun it is to simply
enjoy nature; the sea even when the water is
freezing, the stars which twinkle and hint at
life beyound ourselves, the earth which
squishes and squelches in my hands,
these are things I enjoy again.

Susan Bourke
Australian writer

God sent childen for another purpose than merely to keep up the race — to enlarge our hearts; and to make us unselfish and full of kindly sympathies and affections; to give our souls higher aims; to call out all our faculties to extended enterprise and exertion; and to bring round our firesides bright faces, happy smiles and loving, tender hearts.

Mary Botham Howitt, 1799-1888
English author

The soul is healed by being with children.

Feodor Dostoevsky, 1821-1881
Russian writer

To talk to a child, to fascinate him, is much more difficult than to win an electoral victory. But it is more rewarding.

Colette, 1873-1954
French writer

It's always been my feeling that God lends you your children until they're about eighteen years old. If you haven't made your points with them by then, it's too late.

Betty Ford, b. 1918
First Lady of the United States of America

We should say to each of them: Do you know what you are? You are a marvel. You are unique . . . You may become a Shakespeare, a Michelangelo, a Beethoven. You have the capacity for anything . . .

Pablo Casals, 1876-1973
Spanish cellist, conductor and composer

What good mothers and fathers instinctively feel like doing for their babies is usually best after all.

Benjamin Spock, 1903-1998
American paediatrician

You are the bows from which your
children as living arrows are sent forth.
The Archer sees the mark upon the path
of the infinite,
And He bends you with His might that
His arrows may go swift and far.
Let your bending in the Archer's
hand be for gladness;
For even as He loves the arrow that flies,
so He loves the bow that is stable.

Kahlil Gibran, 1883-1931
Lebanese poet, artist and mystic

I think it must be written somewhere that
the virtues of the mother shall be
visited on the children.

Charles Dickens, 1812-1870
English novelist

My mother was the making of me. She was
so true, so sure of me, and I felt that
I had someone to live for; someone
I must not disappoint.

Thomas Edison, 1847-1931
American inventor

All that I am or hope to be,
I owe to my mother.

Abraham Lincoln, 1809-1865
American statesman and President

My mother had a great deal of trouble with
me, but I think she enjoyed it.

Mark Twain, 1835-1910
American humorist and writer

Mother is the name for God in the lips and
hearts of little children.

William Makepeace Thackeray, 1811-1863
English writer

The mother's heart is the child's school room.

Henry Beecher Ward, 1818-1887
American clergyman and writer

To bring up a child in the way he should go,
travel that way yourself once in a while.

Josh Billings, 1818-1885
American humorist

If a child lives with approval,
He learns to like himself.

Dorothy Law Nolte
American poet

There are two lasting legacies we can
hope to give to our children. One of
these is roots; the other, wings.

Anonymous

When I was a boy of fourteen, my father was
so ignorant I could hardly stand to have the old
man around. But when I got to be twenty-one,
I was astonished at how much he had learned
in seven years.

Mark Twain, 1835-1910
American humorist and writer

I'm doing this for my father. I'm quite happy
that they see me as my father's daughter. My
only concern is that I prove worthy of him.

Aung San Suu Kyi, b. 1945
Burma's democratically elected leader,
winner of Nobel Peace Prize and daughter of
Burma's hero Aung San

Choice

You don't get to choose how you're going
to die. Or when. You can decide how
you're going to live now.

Joan Baez, b. 1941
American folksinger

Choice, not chance, determines destiny.

Anonymous

Few people make a deliberate choice between
good and evil; the choice is between what we
want to do and what we ought to do.

Anonymous

In any moment of decision, the best thing
you can do is the right thing, the next best
thing is the wrong thing, and the worst
thing is to do nothing.

Theodore Roosevelt, 1858-1919
President of the United States of America

He who deliberates at length before taking a single step will spend his whole life on one leg.

Chinese proverb

Civility

A drop of honey catches more flies than a gallon of gall.

Abraham Lincoln, 1809-1865
American statesman and President

Civility costs nothing and buys everything.

Lady Mary Wortley Montague, 1689-1762
British poet and writer

If a man is gracious and courteous to strangers, it shows he is a citizen of the world.

Francis Bacon, 1561-1626
British philosopher, essayist and courtier

The great secret, Eliza, is not having bad manners or good manners, or any particular sort of manners, but having the same manner for all human souls . . .

George Bernard Shaw, 1856-1950
Irish dramatist, writer and critic

[Pygmalion]

They say courtesy is contagious.
So why not start an epidemic?

Anonymous

Punctuality is the politeness of kings.

Louis XV111, 1755-1824
King of France

Comforting Words

Master, what is the best way to
meet the loss of someone we love?
By knowing that when we truly love, it is never
lost. It is only after death that the depth of the
bond is truly felt, and our loved one becomes
more a part of us than was possible in life.

Oriental tradition

Do but consider, however, if we live apart, as
we must, it is much the same whether I am
hundreds or thousands of miles distant from
you. The same Providence will watch over us
there as here. The sun that shines on you will
also afford me the benefit of its cheering rays.

Elizabeth Macarthur, 1767-1850
English-born wife of John Macarthur, founder of
the Australian wool industry, in a letter to her
mother in England

And remember, we all stumble,
every one of us. That's why it's a
comfort to go hand in hand.

E. K. Brough
American writer

For the winter is past,
the rain is over and gone.
The flowers are springing up and the time
of the singing of the birds has come.
Yes, spring is here.

Song of Solomon 2: 11-12

Communication

Starting with self-communication in
private, you can then develop your ability
to communicate with others. Being clear
with yourself opens the way for being
more clear with others about how you
feel and think, enriching your relationships
and social interactions.

Lucia Capacchione
American art therapist and pioneer in inner healing

Use what language you will, you can never say anything to others but what you are.

Ralph Waldo Emerson, 1803-1882
American essayist, poet and philosopher

Only connect!

E. M. Forster, 1879-1970
English novelist

How wonderful it is to say the right thing at the right time. A good man thinks before he speaks; the evil man pours out his evil words without a thought.

Proverbs 15:23, 28

Give every man thy ear, but few thy voice.

William Shakespeare, 1564-1616
English playwright and poet

Speaking without thinking is like shooting without taking aim.

Spanish proverb

Compassion

Compassion is not a sloppy, sentimental feeling for people who are underprivileged or sick . . . it is an absolutely practical belief that, regardless of a person's background, ability or ability to pay, he should be provided with the best that society has to offer.

Neil Kinnock. b. 1942
Welsh politician

When a man has pity on all living creatures then only is he noble.

Buddha, c. 563-483 BC
Indian religious leader and founder of Buddhism

By compassion we make others' misery our own, and so, by relieving them, we relieve ourselves also.

Thomas Browne, 1605-1682
English author and physician

Conscience

The one thing that doesn't abide by majority rule is a person's conscience.

Harper Lee, b. 1926
American novelist

A good conscience is a soft pillow.

German proverb

Keep pace with the drummer you hear, however measured or far away.

Henry David Thoreau, 1817-1862
American essayist, poet and mystic

The voice of conscience is so delicate that it is easy to stifle it: but it is also so clear that it is impossible to mistake it.

Mme Anne de Staël, 1766-1817
Swiss-born French writer

Better to stand ten thousand sneers than one abiding pang, such as time could not abolish, of bitter self-reproach.

Thomas de Quincey, 1785-1859
English essayist

Some good must come by clinging to the right. Conscience is a man's compass, and though the needle sometimes deviates, though one perceives irregularities in directing one's course by it, still one must try to follow its direction.

Vincent Van Gogh, 1853-1890
Dutch post-impressionist painter

He that loses his conscience has nothing left that is worth keeping.

Isaak Walton, 1593-1683
English writer

A peace above all earthly dignities,
A still and quiet conscience.

William Shakespeare, 1564-1616
English playwright and poet

Contentment

To be content, look backward on those who possess less than yourself, not forward on those who possess more.

Benjamin Franklin, 1706-1790
American statesman and scientist

A person who is not disturbed by the incessant flow of desires can alone achieve peace, and not the man who strives to satisfy such desires.

Bhagavad Gita

Health is the greatest gift, contentment the greatest wealth, faithfulness the best relationship.

Buddha. c. 563-483 BC
Indian religious leader, founder of Buddhism

He is richest who is content with the least, for content is the wealth of nature.

Socrates, 468-399 BC
Greek philosopher

Conversation

Conversation. What is it? A mystery! It's the art of never seeming bored, of touching everything with interest, of pleasing with trifles, of being fascinating with nothing at all. How do we define this lively darting about with words, of hitting them back and forth, this short brief smile of ideas which should be conversation?

Guy de Maupassant, 1850-1893
French writer

Ideal conversation must be an exchange of thought, and not, as many of those who worry most about their shortcomings believe, an eloquent exhibition of wit or oratory.

Emily Post, 1873-1960
American etiquette writer

Good nature is more agreeable in conversation than wit and gives a certain air to the countenance which is more amiable than beauty.

Joseph Addison, 1672-1719
English essayist

Conversation has a kind of charm about it, an insinuating and insidious something that elicits secrets from us just like love or liquor.

Seneca, c. 4 BC-65 AD
Roman philosopher, dramatist, poet and statesman

For one word a man is often declared to be wise, and for one word he can be judged to be foolish. We should be careful indeed what we say.

Confucius, c. 550-c. 478 BC
Chinese philosopher

That is the happiest conversation where there is no competition, no vanity, but a calm quiet interchange of sentiments.

Samuel Johnson, 1709-1784
English lexicographer, essayist and wit

Courage

I am not afraid of storms for I am
learning to sail my ship.

Louisa May Alcott, 1832-1888
American novelist

Life shrinks or expands in proportion
to one's courage.

Anaïs Nin, 1903-1977
French novelist

Fearlessness may be a gift, but perhaps
more precious is the courage acquired through
endeavour, courage that come from cultivating
the habit of refusing to let fear dictate one's
actions, courage that could be described as
'grace under pressure' — grace which is
renewed repeatedly in the face of harsh,
unremitting pressure.

Aung San Suu Kyi, b. 1945
*Burma's democratically elected leader and winner of
Nobel Peace Prize*

Courage is the price that life
    extracts for granting peace.
The soul that knows it not, knows
    no release
From little things,
Knows not the livid loneliness of fear
Nor mountain heights where
    bitter joy can hear
The sound of wings.

Amelia Earhart, 1898-1937
American aviator

A light supper, a good night's sleep, and
a fine morning have sometimes made a hero
of the same man who, by an indigestion, a
restless night and a rainy morning, would
have proved a coward.

Lord Chesterfield, 1694-1773
English statesman

Never bend your head, always hold it high.
Look the world in the face.

Helen Keller, 1880-1968
Blind and deaf American writer and scholar

I wanted you to see what real courage is, instead of getting the idea that courage is a man with a gun in his hand. It's when you know you're licked before you begin but you begin anyway and you see it through no matter what.

Harper Lee, b. 1926
American novelist

My message to you is:
Be courageous!
Be as brave as your fathers before you.
Have faith!
Go forward.

Thomas Edison, 1847-1931
American inventor

Facing it, always facing it, that's the way to get through. Face it.

Joseph Conrad, 1856-1924
Polish-born British writer

Courage faces fear and thereby masters it.
Cowardice represses fear and is thereby
mastered by it.

Martin Luther King, Jr, 1929-1968
American civil rights leader and minister

It's better to be a lion for a day than
a sheep all your life.

Sister Elizabeth Kenny, 1866-1952
Australian nurse and pioneer in polio treatment

I hate a fellow whom pride, or cowardice, or
laziness drives into a corner, and who does
nothing when he is there but sit and growl;
let him come out as I do, and bark.

Samuel Johnson, 1709-1784
English lexicographer, essayist and wit

The bravest thing you can do when you are not
brave is to profess courage and act accordingly.

Corra May White Harris, 1869-1935
American writer

No coward soul is mine,
No trembler in the world's
  storm-troubled sphere;
I see Heaven's glory shine,
And faith shines equal, arming
  me from fear.

Emily Brontë,1818-1848
British novelist and poet

Strength alone knows courage. Weakness is
below even defeat, and is born vanquished.

Anne Sophie Swetchine, 1782-1857
Russian writer

I count he braver who overcomes his desires
than he who overcomes his enemies.

Aristotle, 384-322 BC
Greek philosopher

Creativity

No matter how old you get, if you can
keep the desire to be creative, you're
keeping the man-child alive.

John Cassavetes
American film director

In every real man a child is hidden
who wants to play.

Friedrich Nietzche, 1844-1900
German philosopher

Art is an essential reminder of what it is
in life that lasts, of why one lives. Art
communicates, celebrates, mourns and
remembers. What else in our lives
can do this?

Bella Lewitzky, b. 1916
American ballet dancer

Poetry ennobles the heart and the eyes,
and unveils the meaning of all things upon
which the heart and the eyes dwell. It discovers
the secret rays of the universe, and restores
us to forgotten paradises.

Dame Edith Sitwell, 1887-1964
English poet

Masterpieces are not single and solitary births;
they are the outcome of many years of thinking
in common, of thinking by the body of
the people, so that the experience of the
mass is behind the single voice.

Virginia Woolf, 1882-1941
English novelist

Creativity is so delicate a flower that praise
tends to make it bloom, while discouragement
often nips it in the bud. Any of us will put
out more and better ideas if our efforts
are appreciated.

Alex F. Osborn, 1888-1966
American advertising director and writer

Crisis

The English word 'crisis' is translated by the Chinese by two little characters; one means 'danger' and the other means 'opportunity'.

Anonymous

Granted that we face a world crisis which often leaves us standing amid the surging murmur of life's restless sea. But every crisis has both its dangers and its opportunities. Each can spell either salvation or doom. In a dark, confused world the spirit of God may yet reign supreme.

Martin Luther King, Jr, 1929-1968
American civil rights leader and minister

Criticism

A true critic ought to dwell upon excellencies
rather than imperfections.

Joseph Addison, 1672-1719
English essayist

There is nothing as easy as denouncing. It don't
take much to see that something is wrong, but
it does take some eyesight to see what will put
it right again.

Will Rogers, 1879-1935
American humorist and writer

Don't find fault. Find a remedy.

Henry Ford, 1863-1947
American car manufacturer

Deal with the faults of others as gently
as your own.

Chinese proverb

Crying

I have always felt sorry for people afraid of feeling, of sentimentality, who are unable to weep with their whole heart. Because those who do not know how to weep do not know how to laugh either.

Golda Meir, 1898-1978
Prime Minister of Israel

We need never be ashamed of our tears.

Charles Dickens, 1812-1870
English writer

'It opens the lungs, washes the countenance, exercises the eyes, and softens down the temper,' said Mr Bumble. 'So cry away.'

Charles Dickens, 1812-1870
[Oliver Twist]

Curiosity

Curiosity will conquer fear even more
than bravery will.

James Stephens, 1882-1950
Irish novelist

Curiosity is the key to creativity.

Akio Morita
Japanese businessman

Curiosity has its own reason for existing . . .
Never lose a holy curiosity.

Albert Einstein, 1877-1955
German-born American physicist

Disinterested intellectual curiosity is the life
blood of real civilisation.

George Macaulay Trevelyan, 1876-1962
British historian

A generous and elevated mind is distinguished by nothing more certainly than an eminent degree of curiosity.

Samuel Johnson, 1709-1784
English lexicographer, essayist and wit

Curiosity is nothing more than freewheeling intelligence.

Anonymous

Those with a lively sense of curiosity learn something new every day of their lives.

Anonymous

D

Death

I think of death as some delightful journey
That I shall take when my tasks are done.

Ella Wheeler Wilcox, 1850-1919
American writer and poet

We sometimes congratulate ourselves at the
moment of waking from a troubled dream; it
may be so the moment after death.

Nathaniel Hawthorne, 1804-1864
American writer

Life is a great surprise. I do not see why death
should not be an even greater one.

Vladimir Nabokov, 1899-1977
Russian-born American novelist

The dead don't die. They look on and help.

D. H. Lawrence, 1855-1930
English writer and poet

Life does not cease to be funny when
people die any more than it ceases to be
serious when people laugh.

George Bernard Shaw, 1856-1950
Irish dramatist, writer and critic

There is no need to be afraid of death. It is not
the end of the physical body that should worry
us. Rather, our concern must be to live while
we're alive — to release our inner selves from
the spiritual death that comes from living
behind a facade designed to conform to
external definitions of who and what we are.

Elisabeth Kübler-Ross, b. 1926
Swiss-born American psychiatrist and writer

The world is the land of the dying; the next is
the land of the living.

Tyron Edwards, 1809-1894
American theologian

You would know the secret of death.
But how shall you find it unless you seek
it in the heart of life?
The owl whose night-bound eyes are blind unto
the day cannot unveil the mystery of light.
If you would indeed behold the spirit of death,
open your heart wide unto the body of life.
For life and death are one,
even as river and sea are one.

Kahlil Gibran, 1883-1931
Lebanese poet, artist and mystic

The gods conceal from men the happiness of
death, that they may endure life.

Lucan, 39-65 AD
Roman poet

Depression

We can be cured of depression in only fourteen days if every day we will try to think of how we can be helpful to others.

Alfred Adler, 1870-1937
Austrian psychiatrist

The best way to cheer yourself up is to cheer someone else up.

Mark Twain, 1835-1910
American humorist and writer

Never give way to melancholy; resist it steadily, for the habit will encroach.

Sydney Smith, 1771-1845
English clergyman essayist and wit

Difficulties

Nothing is easy to the unwilling.

Thomas Fuller, 1608-1661
English clergyman and writer

The difficulties of life are meant to make us
better, not bitter.

Anonymous

Tackle any difficulty at first sight because the
longer you leave it the larger it grows.

Anonymous

Do what is easy as if it were difficult,
and what is difficult as if it were easy.

Baltasar Gracian, 1601-1658
Spanish writer and priest

Disappointment

Disappointment should be cremated, not embalmed.

Henry S. Haskins
American writer

Disappointment is often the salt of life.

Theodore Parker, 1810-1860
American Unitarian minister

Wisdom comes by disillusionment.

George Santayana, 1863-1952
Spanish philosopher and writer

Nothing worthwhile is achieved without patience, labour and disappointment.

Anonymous

Doubt

If a man will begin with certainties, he shall
end in doubts. But if he will be content to
begin with doubts, he shall end in certainties.

Francis Bacon, 1561-1626
British philosopher, essayist and courtier

Doubt is often the beginning of wisdom.

M. Scott Peck, b. 1936
American psychiatrist and writer

Doubt is an incitation to think.

Anonymous

Dreams

Always live your life with one more dream to fulfil. No matter how many of your dreams you have realised in the past, always have a dream to go. Because when you stop dreaming, life becomes a mundane existence.

Sara Henderson, b. 1936
Australian outback station manager and writer

It seems to me we can never give up longing and wishing while we are thoroughly alive. There are certain things we feel to be beautiful and good, and we must hunger after them.

George Eliot (Mary Ann Evans), 1819-1880
English novelist

I like the dreams of the future better than the history of the past.

Thomas Jefferson, 1743-1826
President of the United States of America

E

Education

Learning . . . should be a joy and full of excitement. It is life's greatest adventure; it is an illustrated excursion into the minds of noble and learned men, not a conducted tour through a jail.

Taylor Caldwell, 1900-1985
American writer

The roots of education are bitter, but the fruit is sweet.

Aristotle, 384-322 BC
Greek philosopher

Give a man a fish and you feed him for a day. Teach a man to fish and you feed him for a lifetime.

Chinese proverb

Learning is the only wealth tyrants cannot despoil. Only death can dim the lamp of knowledge that is within you. The true wealth of a nation lies not in its gold or silver but in its learning, wisdom and in the uprightness of its sons.

Kahlil Gibran, 1883-1931
Lebanese poet, artist and mystic

If a man empties his purse into his head, no one can take it from him.

Benjamin Franklin, 1706-1790
American statesman and scientist

For as the old saying is,
When house and land are gone and spent
Then learning is most excellent.

Samuel Foote, 1720-1777
English actor, dramatist and wit

Train a child in the way he should go, and when he is old he will not depart from it.

Proverbs, 12:4

The primary purpose of a liberal education is to make one's mind a pleasant place in which to spend one's leisure.

Sydney J. Harris, b. 1911
American journalist

The supreme end of education is expert discernment in all things — the power to tell the good from the bad, the genuine from the counterfeit, and to prefer the good and genuine to the bad and counterfeit.

Samuel Johnson, 1709-1784
English lexicographer, essayist and wit

What you teach your children is what you *really* believe in.

Cathy Warner Weatherford, b. 1951
American educator

Education should be gentle and stern, not cold and lax.

Joseph Joubert, 1754-1824
French writer and moralist

Effort

I loathe drudgery as much as any man, but I have learned that the only way to conquer drudgery is to get through it as neatly, as efficiently, as one can. You know perfectly well that a dull job slackly done becomes twice as dull; whereas a dull job which you try to do just as well as you can becomes half as dull. Here again, effort appears to me the main art of living.

Harold Nicolson, 1886-1968
Diplomat, politician, writer and diarist

It takes less time to do a thing right than it does to explain why you did it wrong.

Henry Wadsworth Longfellow, 1807-1882
American poet and writer

Whatever is worth doing is worth doing well.

Lord Chesterfield, 1694-1773
English statesman

Empowerment

My will shall shape my future. Whether I fail or succeed shall be no man's doing but my own. I am the force. I can clear any obstacle before me or I can be lost in the maze. My choice; my responsibility; win or lose, only I hold the key to my destiny.

Elaine Maxwell
American writer

It isn't until you come to a spiritual understanding of who you are — not necessarily a religious feeling, but deep down, the spirit within — that you can begin to take control.

Oprah Winfrey, b. 1954
American television personality

Most powerful is he who has control over himself.

Seneca, 4 BC- AD 65
Roman philosopher, dramatist, poet and statesman

Never doubt that a small group of thoughtful committed citizens can change the world. Indeed, it is the only thing that ever has.

Margaret Mead, 1901-1978
American anthropologist and writer

One oral utterance, which boldly states how you want your life to be, is worth more than a dozen books read or lectures attended. Spoken words describing the good you want, help you to claim it and release it into your own life quickly.

Catherine Ponder
American motivational writer

I am only one; but still I am one. I cannot do everything, but still I can do something; I will not refuse to do the something I can do.

Helen Keller, 1880-1968
Blind and deaf American writer and scholar

Encouragement

Correction does much but encouragement
does more.

Johann von Goethe, 1749-1832
German writer, dramatist and scientist

It must be tempting to succumb to what I call
the FUD factor. I know because I've been
there. The Fear, Uncertainty and Doubt is only
put there by the detractors and critics who
don't know you anyway. You are there because
you are the best and they are not, remember
that. I know you will ignore the distractions.
FOCUS on the job at hand, and
CONCENTRATE on yours and the team's
GOALS (in that order). You will succeed
because you have what it takes . . .

Kieren Perkins, b. 1973
Australian Olympic swimming gold medallist
From a fax in June 1997 to Mark Taylor, Australian
cricket captain 1994-1999

I don't blame the system for my mistakes,
I blame myself . . . Right now I'm being
offered six potentially wonderful pictures. I
think I'm a good example for anyone who
thinks their situation is hopeless. Keep putting
one foot in front of the other, keep showing
up, and you can turn it around.

John Frankenheimer
American film director

Enouragement is like premium gasoline. It
helps to take the knock out of living.

Anonymous

A few words of encouragement can
sometimes tip the scales between another's
failure or success.

Anonymous

Enjoyment

Our wealth lies not in what we have
but in what we enjoy.

Anonymous

True enjoyment comes from activity of
the mind and exercise of the body; the two
are ever united.

Alexander von Humboldt, 1769-1859
German statesman, naturalist and writer

Why not learn to enjoy the little things?
There are so many of them.

Anonymous

The good things of life were meant to
be enjoyed.

Anonymous

Enthusiasm

Every great and commanding movement in the annals of the world is a triumph of enthusiasm.

Ralph Waldo Emerson. 1803-1882
American essayist, poet and philosopher

You must learn day by day, year by year, to broaden your horizon. The more things you love, the more you are interested in, the more you enjoy, the more you are indignant about, the more you have left when anything happens.

Ethel Barrymore, 1879-1959
American actress

If it were as easy to arouse enthusiasm as it is suspicion, just think what could be accomplished.

Anonymous

You can do anything if you have enthusiasm. Enthusiasm is the yeast that makes your hopes rise to the stars. Enthusiasm is the spark in your eye, the swing in your gait, the grip of your hand, the irresistible surge of your will and your energy to execute your ideas. Enthusiasts are fighters, they have fortitude, they have staying qualities. Enthusiasm is at the bottom of all progress! With it, there is accomplishment. Without it, there are only alibis.

Henry Ford, 1863-1947
American car manufacturer

We could hardly wait to get up in the morning!

Wilbur Wright, 1867-1912 and
Orville Wright , 1871-1948
American inventors

Just don't give up trying what what you really want to do. Where there is love and inspiration, I don't think you can go wrong.

Ella Fitzgerald, 1918-1996
American singer

Let your enthusiasm radiate in your voice, your actions, your facial expressions, your personality, the words you use, and the thoughts you think! Nothing great was ever achieved without enthusiasm.

Ralph Waldo Emerson, 1803-1882
American essayist, poet and philosopher

Love the moment, and the energy of that moment will spread beyond all boundaries.

Corita Kent, b. 1918
American graphic artist

Nothing is so contagious as enthusiasm . . . It is the genius of sincerity and truth accomplishes no victories without it.

Edward Bulwer-Lytton, 1803-1873
British novelist and politician

Epitaphs

She would rather light a candle than curse the darkness, and her glow has warmed the earth.

Adlai Stevenson, 1900-1965
American lawyer, statesman and
United Nations ambassador

[Written on the death of Eleanor Roosevelt]

The friend of man, the friend of truth;
The friend of age, the guide of youth;
If there's another world, he lives in bliss;
If there is none, he made the best of this.

Robert Burns, 1759-1796
Scottish poet

[Epistle to the Rev. John McMath]

You could write a list of epitaphs which describe a perfect life. They describe Peter's [Peter Cook's] perfectly.

1. He added to the sum of human happiness.
2. He never harmed anyone but himself.
3. He left the world a better place than he found it.
4. He never achieved anything at the expense of anyone else.
5. He made innumerable friends, but not one enemy.
6. He never complained.
7. He was never mean, boastful, envious or vain.
8. He never told anyone else how to behave.
9. He never betrayed a confidence.
10. He made people laugh.

God bless him.

Stephen Fry, b. 1947
English actor, comedian and writer

[Peter Cook Remembered]

Error

Truth emerges more readily from error than
from confusion.

Francis Bacon, 1561-1626
British philosopher, essayist and courtier

Things could be worse. Suppose your errors
were counted and published every day like
those of a baseball player.

Anonymous

Great services are not cancelled by one act or
by one single errror.

Benjamin Disraeli, 1804-1881
British Prime Minister and writer

An error doesn't become a mistake until you
refuse to correct it.

Anonymous

Excellence

The secret of joy in work is contained in one word — excellence. To know how to do something well is to enjoy it.

Pearl S. Buck, 1892-1972
American writer and missionary

Excuses

Excuses fool no one but the person
who makes them.

Anonymous

The man who really wants to do something
finds a way; the other man makes an excuse.

Anonymous

Experience

The best advice you'll get is from someone who has made the same mistake himself.

Anonymous

Experience is the child of Thought, and Thought is the child of Action.

Benjamin Disraeli, 1804-1881
British Prime Minister and writer

There are many truths of which the full meaning cannot be realised until personal experience has brought it home.

John Stuart Mill, 1806-1873
English philosopher, reformer and politician

Experience is the wisdom that enables us to recognise the folly that we have already embraced.

Ambrose Bierce, 1842-1914
American journalist

We should be careful to get out of experience only the wisdom that is in it — and stop there; lest we be like the cat that sits down on the stove-lid. She will never sit down on a hot stove-lid again — and that is well; but also she will never sit down on a cold one anymore.

Mark Twain, 1835-1910
American humorist and writer

Experience is a good teacher, but she sends in terrific bills.

Minna Antrim, 1861-1950
American writer

The least expensive education is to learn from the mistakes of others.

Anonymous

F

Failure

The difference between failure and success
is doing a thing nearly right and doing
a thing exactly right.

Anonymous

Our greatest glory is not in never falling, but in
rising every time we fall.

Confucius, c. 550-478 BC
Chinese philosopher

We have forty million reasons for failure, but
not a single excuse.

Rudyard Kipling, 1865-1936
Indian-born British poet and writer

Failure is the line of least persistence.

Anonymous

Only those who dare to fail greatly can ever achieve greatly.

Robert F. Kennedy, 1925-1968
American lawyer and politician

Nothing is ever entirely wrong. Even a broken clock is right twice a day.

Anonymous

Good people are good because they've come to wisdom through failure.

William Saroyan, 1908-1981
American writer and dramatist

My downfall raises me to great heights.

Napoleon Bonaparte, 1769-1821
French emperor and general

There is no failure except in not trying.

Elbert Hubbard, 1856-1915
American writer

Faith

I believe that God is in me as the sun is in the colour and fragrance of a flower — the light in my darkness, the voice in my silence.

Helen Keller, 1880-1968
Blind and deaf American writer and scholar

Let nothing disturb you. Let nothing frighten you. Everything passes away except God.

St Theresa, 1515-1582
Spanish nun

The reason why birds can fly and we can't is simply that they have perfect faith, for to have faith is to have wings.

J. M. Barrie, 1860-1937
Scottish writer and dramatist

Faith is the subtle chain
Which binds us to the infinite; the voice
Of deep life within, that will remain
Until we crowd it thence.

Elizabeth Oakes Smith, 1806-1893
American writer

Blessed are they they that have not seen, and
yet have believed.

John 20:29

I pray hard, work hard and leave
the rest to God.

Florence Griffith Joyner, b. 1953
American track athlete

I am positive I have a soul; nor can all the
books with which the materialists have
pestered the world ever convince me of
the contrary.

Laurence Sterne, 1713-1768
Irish-born British writer

Yes, I have doubted. I have wandered off the
path. I have been lost. But I always returned. It
is beyond the logic I seek. It is intuitive — an
intrinsic, built-in sense of direction. I seem to
find my way home. My faith has wavered but
has saved me.

Helen Hayes, 1900-1993
American actress

We live in a scary horrible world now, with murder, war, poverty, hunger. I think people need to be reassured there is a higher meaning to all this chaos.

Nina Sodowski
American film producer

Faith is the bird that feels the light when the dawn is dark.

Rabindranath Tagore, 1861-1941
Indian poet and philosopher

The suffering and agonising moments through which I have passed over the last few years have also drawn me closer to God. More than ever before I am convinced of the reality of a personal God.

Martin Luther King, Jr, 1929-1968
American civil rights leader and minister

Reason is itself a matter of faith. It is an act of faith to assert that our thoughts have any relation to reality at all.

G. K. Chesterton, 1874-1936
English writer and critic

Faith builds a bridge across the gulf of death,
To break the shock blind nature cannot shun,
And lands thought smoothly on the farther shore.

Edward Young, 1683-1765
English poet, dramatist and clergyman

With faith, man can achieve anything. Faith is the foundation for the realisation of God.

Sai Baba
Indian spiritual master

Faults

The greatest fault is to be conscious of none.

Thomas Carlyle, 1795-1881
Scottish historian, essayist and critic

We must touch his weaknesses with a delicate hand. There are some faults so nearly allied to excellence, that we can scarce weed out the fault without eradicating the virtue.

Oliver Goldsmith, 1728-1774
British writer

A man's faults are the faults of his time, while his virtues are his own.

Johann von Goethe, 1749-1832
German writer, dramatist and scientist

Always acknowledge a fault frankly. This will throw those in authority off their guard and give you opportunity to commit more.

Mark Twain, 1835-1910
American humorist and writer

Fear

I have not ceased being fearful, but I have ceased to let fear control me. I have accepted fear as a part of life — specifically the fear of change, the fear of the unknown; and I have gone ahead despite the pounding in my heart that says: turn back, you'll die if you venture too far.

Erica Jong, b. 1942
American author

Fear: the best way out is through.

Helen Keller, 1880-1968
Blind and deaf American writer and scholar

I believe anyone can conquer fear by doing the things he fears to do, provided he keeps doing them until he gets a record of successful experiences behind him.

Eleanor Roosevelt, 1884-1962
*First Lady of the United States of America,
writer and diplomat*

Fear is an emotion indispensable for survival.

Hannah Arendt, 1906-1975
German-born American political philosopher

Fear is a question. What are you afraid of and why? Our fears are a treasure house of self knowledge if we explore them.

Marilyn French, b. 1929
American novelist

Within a system which denies the existence of basic human rights, fear tends to be the order of the day. Fear of imprisonment, fear of torture, fear of death, fear of losing friends, family, property or means of livelihood, fear of poverty, fear of isolation, fear of failure . . . Yet even under the most crushing state machinery, courage rises up again and again, for fear is not the natural state of civilised man.

Aung San Suu Kyi, b. 1945
Burma's democratically elected leader and Nobel Peace Prize winner

Avoiding danger is no safer in the long run than outright exposure. The fearful are caught as often as the bold.

Helen Keller, 1880-1968
Blind and deaf American writer and scholar

It is not death that a man should fear, but he should fear never beginning to live.

Marcus Aurelius, 121-180 AD
Roman emperor and philosopher

Fools & Foolishness

The greatest lesson in life is to know that even fools are right sometimes.

Winston Churchill, 1874-1965
British statesman and Prime Minister

Each day, and the living of it, has to be a conscious creation in which discipline and order are relieved with some play and pure foolishness.

May Sarton, 1912-1995
American writer

Mix a little foolishness with your serious plans;
it's wonderful to be silly at the right moment.

Horace, 65-8 BC
Roman poet

If people didn't sometimes do silly things,
nothing intelligent would ever get done.

Ludwig Wittgenstein, 1889-1952
Austrian-born English philosopher

A little nonsense now and then
Is relished by the best of men.

Anonymous

Let us be grateful for the fools. But for them
the rest of us could not succeed.

Mark Twain, 1835-1910
American humorist and writer

Forgiveness

Good, to forgive,
Best, to forget!
Living, we fret;
Dying, we live.

Robert Browning, 1812-1889
English poet

Forgiveness is the key to action and freedom.

Hannah Arendt, 1906-1975
German-born American political philosopher

A quarrel between friends, when made up,
adds a new tie to friendship, as experience
shows that the callosity formed round a broken
bone makes it stronger than before.

St Francis de Sales, 1567-1622
French theologian

For my part I believe in the forgiveness of sins
and the redemption of ignorance.

Adlai Stevenson, 1900-1965
American lawyer, statesman and
United Nations representative

Forgive us our trespasses as we forgive them
that trespass against us.

The Lord's Prayer

The man who opts for revenge should
dig two graves.

Chinese proverb

He that cannot forgive others breaks the bridge
over which he must pass himself; for every
man has need to be forgiven.

Thomas Fuller, 1608-1661
English clergyman and writer

It is very easy to forgive others their mistakes;
it takes more grit and gumption to forgive
them for having witnessed your own.

Jessamyn West, 1907-1984
American writer

Forgiveness is not an occasional act, it is a
permanent attitude.

Martin Luther King, Jr, 1929-1968
American civil rights leader and minister

Freedom

In the future days, which we seek to make
secure, we look forward to a world founded
upon four essential freedoms. The first is
freedom of speech and expression —
everywhere in the world. The second is
freedom of every person to worship God in
his own way — everywhere in the world.
The third is freedom from want . . .
The fourth is freedom from fear.

Franklin D. Roosevelt, 1882-1945
President of the United States of America

To be free is to have achieved your life.

Tennessee Williams, 19ll-1983
American dramatist

Where the spirit of the Lord is, there is liberty.

11 Corinthians, 3:17

They that can give up essential liberty to obtain a little temporary safety deserve neither liberty nor safety.

Benjamin Franklin, 1706-1790
American statesman and scientist

Free choice is the greatest gift God gives to his children.

Elisabeth Kübler-Ross, b. 1926
Swiss-born American psychiatrist

I wish that every human life might be pure transparent freedom.

Simone de Beauvoir, 1908-1986
French writer

To move freely you must be deeply rooted.

Bella Lewitzky, b. 1916
American ballet dancer

Every human being has the liberty to do that which is good, just and honest.

Anonymous

Freedom ends when it begins to deprive
another of his freedom.

Anonymous

Liberty is not a means to a higher political end.
It is itself the highest political end.

Lord Acton, 1834-1902

British political philosopher and historian

The hope of the world is still in dedicated
minorities. The trail-blazers in human,
academic, scientific and religious freedom
have always been in the minority.

Martin Luther King, Jr, 1929-1968
American civil rights leader and minister

Friendship

We are all travellers in the wilderness of this world, and the best we can find in our travels is an honest friend.

Robert Louis Stevenson, 1850-1894
Scottish writer and poet

True happiness consists not in the multitude of friends but in the worth and choice.

Ben Jonson, c. 1573-1637
English dramatist and poet

Friendship is a divine elixir that draws you towards people and allows you to spread yourself further.

Deborah Forster
Australian journalist

A real friend will tell you when you have spinach stuck in your teeth.

Anonymous

I have learned that to have a good friend is the purest of all God's gifts, for it is a love that has no exchange or payment.

Frances Farmer, 1910-1970
American actress and writer

I want someone to laugh with me, someone to be grave with me, someone to please me and help my discrimination with his or her own remark, and at times, no doubt, to admire my acuteness and penetration.

Robert Burns, 1759-1796
Scottish poet

The antidote for fifty enemies is one friend.

Aristotle, 384-322 BC
Greek philosopher

A real friend is one who walks in when the rest of the world walks out.

Walter Winchell, 1879-1972
American journalist

Friendship improves happiness and abates misery by doubling our joy and dividing our grief.

Joseph Addison, 1672-1719
English essayist

It is one of the blessings of friends that you can afford to be stupid with them.

Ralph Waldo Emerson, 1803-1882
American essayist, poet and philosopher

Fame is the scentless sunflower, with gaudy crown of gold;
But friendship is the breathing rose, with sweets in every fold.

Oliver Wendell Holmes, 1809-1894
American writer and physician

You can make more friends in two months by becoming interested in other people than you can in two years by trying to get other people interested in you.

Dale Carnegie, 1888-1955
American writer and lecturer

Friendship with oneself is all-important
because without it one cannot be friends
with anyone else in the world.

Eleanor Roosevelt, 1884-1962
*First Lady of the United States of America, writer and
diplomat*

For whoever knows how to return a kindness
he has received must be a friend above price.

Sophocles, 496-406 BC
Greek tragedian

The best mirror is an old friend.

English proverb

Anyone can sympathise with the sufferings of a
friend, but it takes a fine nature to sympathise
with a friend's success.

Oscar Wilde, 1854-1900
Irish playright, novelist and wit

If you have a friend worth loving
Love him. Yes, and let him know
That you love him, ere life's evening
Tinge his brow with sunset's glow;
Why should good words ne'er be said
Of a friend until he is dead?

Daniel W. Hoyt
Poet

I always felt that the great high privilege, relief
and comfort of friendship was that one had to
explain nothing.

Katherine Mansfield, 1888-1923
New Zealand short story writer

Under the magnetism of friendship the modest
man becomes bold; the shy, confident; the lazy,
active; or the impetuous, prudent and peaceful.

William Makepeace Thackeray, 1811-1863
English writer

True friendship is a plant of slow growth and must undergo and withstand the shocks of adversity before it is entitled to the appellation.

George Washington, 1732-1799
President of the United States of America

A friendship counting nearly forty years is the finest kind of shade-tree I know.

James Russell Lowell, 1819-1891
American poet and diplomat

Oh, the inexpressible comfort of feeling safe with a person; having neither to weigh thoughts nor measure words, but pour them all out, as they are, chaff and grain together, knowing that a faithful hand will take and sift them, keep what is worth keeping, and then, with the breath of kindness, blow the rest away.

Geoge Eliot (Mary Ann Evans), 1819-1880
English novelist

The truth is friendship is every bit as sacred and eternal as marriage.

Katherine Mansfield, 1888-1923
New Zealand short story writer

Old books, old wine, old Nankin blue,
All things, in short, to which belong
The charm, the grace, that Time makes
    strong — All these I prize, but
    (entre nous)
Old friends are best!

Henry Austin Dobson, 1840-1921
English poet

Life is nothing without friendship.

Cicero, 106-43 BC
Roman orator

To know someone here or there with whom
you feel there is understanding in spite of
distances or thoughts unexpressed — that can
make of this earth a garden.

Johann von Goethe, 1749-1832
German writer, dramatist and scientist

Think where man's glory most begins
    and ends,
And say that my glory was I had such
    friends.

W. B. Yeats, 1865-1939
Irish poet, dramatist and writer

We take care of our health, we lay up money, we make our room tight, and our clothing sufficient; but who provides wisely that he shall not be wanting in the best property of all — friends?

Ralph Waldo Emerson, 1803-1882
American essayist, poet and philosopher

If a man does not make new acquaintance as he advances through life, he will soon find himself alone. A man, sir, should keep his friendship in constant repair.

Samuel Johnson, 1709-1784
English lexicographer, essayist and wit

A friend is a present which you give yourself.

Robert Louis Stevenson, 1850-1894
Scottish writer and poet

One's friends are that part of the human race with which one can be human.

George Santayana, 1863-1952
Spanish philosopher and writer

It is the friends that you can call
at 4 a.m. that matter.

Marlene Dietrich, 1901-1992
German actress and singer

A friend is someone with whom I may be
sincere. Before him I may think aloud.

Ralph Waldo Emerson, 1803-1882
American essayist, poet and philosopher

Friendship gilds prosperity and lessens adversity
by dividing and sharing it.

Cicero, 106-43 BC
Roman orator

The most I can do for my friend is simply to
be his friend. I have not wealth to bestow
on him. If he knows that I am happy in
loving him, he will want no other reward.
Is not friendship divine in this?

Henry David Thoreau, 1817-1862
American essayist, poet and mystic

Let there be no purpose in friendship save
the deepening of the spirit.
For love that seeks aught but the disclosure
of its own mystery is not love but a
net cast forth, and only the unprofitable
is caught . . .
And in the sweetness of friendship
let there be laughter, and sharing of
pleasures.
For in the dew of little things the heart
finds its morning and is refreshed.

Kahlil Gibran, 1883-1931
Lebanese poet, artist and mystic

A companion loves some agreeable qualities
which a man may possess, but a friend loves
the man himself.

James Boswell, 1740-1795
Scottish lawyer and diarist

When befriended, remember it; when you
befriend, forget it.

Benjamin Franklin, 1706-1790
American statesman and scientist

Love is like the wild rose-briar;
Friendship like the holly tree.
The holly is dark when the rose-briar
  blooms,
But which one blooms most constantly?

Emily Brontë, 1818-1848
English novelist and poet

Life is to be fortified by many friendships.
To love and be loved is the greatest
happiness of existence.

Sydney Smith, 1771-1845
English clergyman, essayist and wit

The glory of friendship is not the outstretched
hand, nor the kindly smile, nor the joy of
companionship; it is the spiritual inspiration
that comes to one when he discovers
that someone else believes in him
and is willing to trust him.

Ralph Waldo Emerson, 1803-1882
American essayist, poet and philosopher

G

Gardens & Gardening

He who plants a garden plants happiness.

Chinese proverb

What makes a garden,
And why do gardens grow?
Love lives in gardens
God and lovers know.

Carolyn Giltinam, early 19th century
English poet

Every time I talk to a savant I feel quite sure
that happiness is no longer a possibility. Yet
when I talk to my gardener, I'm convinced of
the opposite.

Bertrand Russell, 1872-1970
English philosopher, mathematician and writer

How to be happy when you are miserable.
Plant Japanese poppies with cornflowers and
mignonette, and bed out the petunias among
the sweet-peas so they shall scent each other.
See the sweet-peas coming up.

Rumer Godden, b. 1907
English writer

God Almighty first planted a garden. And indeed it is the purest of human pleasures.

Francis Bacon, 1561-1626
English philosopherand courtier

Proceed my Friend, pursue thy healthful
    toil.
Dispose thy ground and meliorate thy soil;
Range thy young plants in walks,
    or clumps, or bow'rs,
Diffuse o'er sunny banks thy fragrant
    flow'rs:
And, while the new creation round
    thee springs,
Enjoy unchecked the guiltless bliss it brings.

John Scott, 1730-1793
British poet

A man has at least made a start in discovering
the meaning of human life when he plants
shade trees under which he knows full well he
will never sit.

D. Elton Trueblood, b. 1900
American Quaker scholar

The planting of trees is the least self-centred of
all that we can do. It is a purer act of faith
than the procreation of children.

Thornton Wilder, 1897-1975
American writer

There is no unbelief:
Whoever plants a seed beneath the sod
And waits to see it push away the clod,
He trusts in God.

Elizabeth York Case, 1840-1911
American writer

Gardening is an act of grace.

May Sarton, 1912-1995
American writer and poet

Genius

A genius! For thirty-seven years I've practised fourteen hours a day, and now they call me a genius!

Pablo Sarasate, 1844-1908
Spanish violinist and composer

The secret of genius is to carry the spirit of the child into old age, which means never losing your enthusiasm.

Aldous Huxley, 1894-1963
English writer

Genius is nothing more than inflamed enthusiasm.

Anonymous

Every production of genius must be the production of enthusiasm.

Benjamin Disraeli, 1804-1881
English statesman and writer

Men give me credit for some genius. All the genius I have is this: When I have a subject in mind, I study it profoundly. Day and night it is before me. My mind becomes pervaded with it ...the effort which I have made is what people are pleased to call the fruit of genius. It is the fruit of labour and thought.

Alexander Hamilton, 1755-1804
American statesman

Often genius is just another way of spelling perseverance.

Anonymous

True genius resides in the capacity for evaluation of uncertain, hazardous and conflicting information.

Winston Churchill, 1874-1965
British statesman and Prime Minister

Everyone is a genius at least once a year; a real genius has his original ideas closer together.

George Lichtenberg, 1742-1799
German physicist, satirist and writer

The highest intellects, like the
tops of mountains, are the first to
reflect the dawn.

Lord Macaulay, 1800-1859
English historian, statesman, essayist and poet

Good sense travels on well-worn paths;
genius never.

Cesar Lombroso, 1836-1909
Italian founder of criminology

If people knew how hard I work to gain my
mastery, it would not seem so wonderful at all.

Michelangelo, 1475-1564
Italian painter and sculptor

Gifts

In all ranks of life the human heart yearns for the beautiful; and the beautiful things that God makes are his gift to all alike.

Harriet Beecher Stowe, 1811-1896
American author and social reformer

When you arise in the morning, think of what a precious privilege it is to be alive — to breathe, to think, to enjoy, to love.

Marcus Aurelius, 121-180 AD
Roman emperor and philosopher

God's gifts put man's best dreams to shame.

Elizabeth Barrett Browning, 1806-1861
English poet

Giving

A bit of fragrance always clings to the hand
that gives you roses.

Chinese proverb

Giving whether it be time, labour, affection,
advice, gifts, or whatever, is one of life's
greatest pleasures.

Rebecca Russell, b. 1905
American writer

You find true joy and happiness in life when
you give and give and go on giving.

Eileen Caddy
Co-founder of the Findhorn Foundation, Scotland

We make a living by what we get, but we make
a life by what we give.

Winston Churchill, 1874-1965
British statesman and Prime Minister

It is well to give when asked, but it is better to give unasked, through understanding.

Kahlil Gibran, 1883-1931
Lebanese poet, artist and mystic

It is more blessed to give than to receive.

Acts of the Apostles, 20:35

Not what we give, but what we share,
For the gift without the giver is bare.

James Russell Lowell, 1819-1891
American poet and diplomat

The love we give away is the only
love we keep.

Elbert Hubbard, 1856-1915
American writer

If there be any truer measure of a man than by what he does, it must be by what he gives.

Robert South, 1634-1716
English Church of England theologian

It is possible to give away and become richer.
It is also possible to hold on too tightly and
lose everything. Yes, the liberal man shall be
rich. By watering others, he waters himself.

Proverbs 11:24, 25

A cheerful giver does not count the cost of
what he gives. His heart is set on pleasing and
cheering him to whom the gift is given.

Julian of Norwich
Revelations of Divine Love

The wise man does not lay up treasure.
The more he gives to others, the more
he has for his own.

Lao-Tze, c. 600 BC
Chinese philosopher and founder of Taoism

The heart of the giver makes the gift
dear and precious.

Martin Luther, 1483-1546
German protestant reformer

He that gives should never remember; he that receives should never forget.

The Talmud

Generosity consists less of giving a great deal than in gifts well timed.

Jean de La Bruyere
French writer

It is more blessed to give than to receive.

Acts: 20:35

The hand that gives, gathers.

English proverb

Goals

I knew I was going to be a comedian when I was about six. You get what you believe you'll get. You have to really want it and you'll get it.

Billy Connolly, b. 1942
Scottish comedian

No bird soars too high if he soars with his own wings.

William Blake, 1757-1827
English poet and artist

Far away there in the sunshine are my highest aspirations. I may not reach them but I can look up and see their beauty, believe in them and try to follow.

Louisa May Alcott, 1832-1888
American novelist

Awake, arise and stop not 'til the goal is reached.

Sai Baba
Indian spiritual leader

When goals go, meaning goes. When meaning goes, purpose goes. When purpose goes, life goes dead on our hands.

Carl Jung, 1875-1961
Swiss psychiatrist

Efforts and courage are not enough without purpose and direction.

John F. Kennedy, 1917-1963
President of the United States of America

The difference between a dream and a goal is a plan.

Anonymous

If you aspire to the highest place, it is no disgrace to stop at the second or even the third place.

Cicero, 106-43 BC
Roman orator, statesman and essayist

Aim at the sun, and you may not reach it; but your arrow will fly far higher than if you aimed at an object on a level with yourself.

Judy Hawes, b. 1913
American children's author

Set your sights high, the higher the better.
Expect the most wonderful things to happen, not in the future but right now.
Realise that nothing is too good.
Allow absolutely nothing to hamper you or hold you up in any way.

Eileen Caddy
Co-founder of the Findhorn Foundation, Scotland

Never look down to test the ground before taking your next step; only he who keeps his eye fixed on the far horizon will find his right road.

Dag Hammarskjold, 1905-1961
Swedish statesman and humanitarian

Good Points

Think of someone you admire very much.
Write down a list of the things you admire
most about this person. You have just listed
your own good points!
Read them through carefully, and give yourself
credit for having these fine qualities.

Anonymous

A man generally has the good or ill qualities he
attributes to mankind.

William Shenstone, 1714-1763
English poet

Goodness

The greatest pleasure I know is to do a good action by stealth, and to have it found out by accident.

Charles Lamb, 1775-1834
British essayist

Waste no more time arguing
what a good man should be. Be one.

Marcus Aurelius, 121-180 AD
Roman emperor and philosopher

True goodness springs from a man's heart. All men are born good.

Confucius, c. 550-c. 478 BC
Chinese philosopher

Good, the more communicated, the more abundant grows.

John Milton, 1608-1674
English poet

It was only when I lay there on rotting prison straw that I sensed within myself the first stirrings of the good. Gradually it was disclosed to me that the line separating good and evil passes, not through states, not between classes, not between political parties either, but right through every human heart and through all human hearts.

Alexander Solzhenitsyn, b. 1918
Russian writer

For the good are always merry,
Save by an evil chance,
And the merry love the fiddle,
And the merry love to dance.

W. B. Yeats, 1865-1939
Irish poet, dramatist and writer

Good is itself, what ever comes.
It grows, and makes, and bravely
Persuades, beyond all tilt of wrong;
Stronger than anger, wiser than strategy,
Enough to subdue cities and men
If we believe it with a long courage
    of truth.

Christopher Fry, b. 1909
English verse dramatist

Greatness

Great men are the guide-posts and landmarks
in the state.

Edmund Burke, 1729-1797
British statesman and philosopher

No great man lives in vain. The history of the
world is but the biography of great men.

Thomas Carlyle, 1795-1881
Scottish historian, essayist and critic

Keep away from people who try to belittle
your ambitions. Small people always do that,
but the really great make you feel that you,
too, can become great.

Mark Twain, 1835-1910
American humorist and writer

Greatness lies not only in being strong, but in
the right use of strength.

Henry Ward Beecher, 1813-1887
American clergyman

I studied the lives of great men and famous women, and I found that the men and women who got to the top were those who did the jobs they had in hand, with everything they had of energy and enthusiasm and hard work.

Harry S. Truman, 1884-1972
President of the United States of America

The heights by great men reached
    and kept
Were not attained by sudden flight,
But they, while their companions slept,
Were toiling upward in the night.

Henry Wadsworth Longfellow, 1807-1882
American poet and writer

The measure of a truly great man is the courtesy with which he treats lesser men.

Anonymous

Great lives never go out. They go on.

Benjamin Harrison, 1833-1901
President of the United States of America

Growth

Growth, in some curious way, I suspect, depends on being always in motion just a little bit, one way or another.

Norman Mailer, b. 1932
American writer

No one remains quite what he was when he recognises himself.

Thomas Mann, 1875-1955
German writer

You must learn day by day, year by year, to broaden your horizons. The more things you love, the more you are interested in, the more you enjoy, the more your are indignant about — the more you have left when anything happens.

Ethel Barrymore, 1879-1959
American actress

Women are always being tested . . . but
ultimately, each of us has to define who we
are individually and then do the very best job
we can to grow into that.

Hillary Clinton
First Lady of the United States of America and lawyer

We learn from experiences, both good and bad,
and with that knowledge comes change . . .
and growth.

Anonymous

Growing up is, after all, only the understanding
that one unique and incredible experience is
what everyone shares.

Doris Lessing, b. 1919
British writer

Life is a lively process of becoming.

General Douglas MacArthur, 1880-1964
American military leader

Who is not satisfied with himself will grow.

Hebrew proverb

Guilt

There's no point in being crippled by guilt.
Simply acknowledge to yourself that you have
done something wrong, learn by it, and get on
with the rest of your life.

Anonymous

Should we all confess our sins to one another
we would all laugh at one another for our lack
of originality.

Kahlil Gibran, 1883-1931
Lebanese poet, artist and mystic

We all feel guilty about something. The
only positive thing about such feelings is that
they help one to change and to behave better
in the future.

Anonymous

H

Habit

Dull habit can rob you of life's rich variety.
Make a point of doing things differently sometimes. Meet some friends for breakfast, get up
early and go for an early morning walk and, in
summer, have a picnic dinner on the beach.
Life will take on a new glow.

Anonymous

Cultivate only the habits that you are willing
should master you.

Elbert Hubbard, 1856-1915
American writer

We must make automatic and habitual, as early
as possible, as many useful actions as we can.

William James, 1842-1910
American psychologist and philosopher

Happiness

Happiness must be cultivated. It is like character. It is not a thing to be safely let alone for a moment, or it will run to weeds.

Elizabeth Stuart Phelps, 1815-1852
American novelist

I don't know what your destiny will be; but one thing I know: the only ones among you who will be really happy are those who will have sought and found how to serve.

Albert Schweitzer, 1875-1965
French medical missionary

The great essentials to happiness in this life are something to do, something to love and something to hope for.

Joseph Addison, 1672-1719
English essayist

Whether happiness may come or not,
one should try and prepare one's self to
do without it.

George Eliot (Mary Ann Evans) 1819-1880
English novelist

Most people are about as happy as they make
up their minds to be.

Abraham Lincoln, 1809-1865
American statesman and President

Cherish all your happy moments: they make a
fine cushion for old age.

Booth Tarkington, 1869-1946
American writer and dramatist

Anything you're good at contributes
to happiness.

Bertrand Russell, 1872-1970
English philosopher, mathematician and writer

If only we'd stop trying to be happy, we could have a pretty good time.

Edith Wharton, 1862-1937
American novelist

Many persons have a wrong idea of what constitutes true happiness. It is not attained through self-gratification but through fidelity to a worthy cause.

Helen Keller, 1880-1968
Blind and deaf American writer and scholar

If you want to understand the meaning of happiness, you must see it as a reward and not as a goal.

Antoine de Saint-Exupery, 1900-1944
French writer and aviator

All who would win joy, must share it; happiness was born to be a twin.

Lord Byron, 1788-1824
English poet

When we cannot find contentment in ourselves, it is useless to seek it elsewhere.

Duc de la Rochefoucauld, 1613-1680
French writer

Happiness arises in the first place from the enjoyment of one's self, and, in the next, from the friendship and conversations of a few select companions.

Joseph Addison, 1672-1719
English essayist

We have no more right to consume happiness without producing it than to consume wealth without producing it.

George Bernard Shaw, 1856-1950
Irish dramatist, writer and critic

There are eight requisites for contented living:

health enough to make work a pleasure,

wealth enough to support your needs,

strength to battle with difficulties and overcome them,

grace enough to confess your sins and forsake them,

patience enough to toil until some good is accomplished,

charity enough to see some good in your neighbour,

faith enough to make real the things of God,

hope enough to remove all anxious fear regarding the future.

Johann von Goethe, 1749-1832
German writer, dramatist and scientist

Happiness is like coke — something you get as a by-product in the process of making something else.

Aldous Huxley, 1894-1964
British novelist

The secret of happiness is not in doing what one likes, but in liking what one has to do.

J. M. Barrie, 1860-1937
Scottish writer and dramatist

Happiness is not best achieved by those who seek it directly.

Bertrand Russell, 1872-1970
British philosopher, mathematician and writer

It is neither wealth, nor splendour but tranquillity and occupation which give happiness.

Thomas Jefferson, 1743-1826
President of the United States of America

Knowledge of what is possible is the beginning of happiness.

George Santayana, 1863-1952
Spanish philosopher and writer

Hate

Hatred rarely does any harm to its object. It is the hater who suffers. His soul is warped and his life poisoned by dwelling on past injuries or projecting schemes of revenge. Rancour in the bosom is the foe of personal happiness.

Lord Beaverbrook, 1879-1964
Canadian-born British newspaper owner and writer

Hate is like acid. It can damage the vessel in which it is stored as well as destroy the object on which it is poured.

Ann Landers, b. 1918
American advice columnist

I have decided to stick with love.
Hate is too great a burden to bear.

Martin Luther King, Jr, 1929-1968
American civil rights leader and minister

If you hate a person, you hate something in him that is part of yourself. What isn't part of ourselves doesn't disturb us.

Herman Hesse, 1877-1962
German novelist and poet

Always remember that others may hate you but those who hate you don't win unless you hate them. And then you destroy yourself.

Richard M. Nixon, 1913-1994
President of the United States of America

Rather perish than hate and fear, and twice rather die than make oneself hated and feared — this must some day become the highest maxim for every single commonwealth.

Friedrich Nietzsche, 1844-1900
German philosopher

I shall never permit myself to sink so low as to hate any man.

Booker T. Washington, 1856-1915
American educator and writer

Health

I am convinced digestion is the great secret of life.

Sydney Smith, 1771-1845
English clergyman, essayist and wit

The Mind is the Key to Health and Happiness.

Sai Baba
Indian spiritual master

Cheerfulness is the best promoter of health and is as friendly to the mind as to the body.

Joseph Addison, 1672-1719
English essayist

O health! health is the blessing of the rich! the riches of the poor! who can buy thee at too dear a rate, since there is no enjoying this world without thee?

Ben Jonson, 1573-1637
English dramatist and poet

One swears by wholemeal bread, one by
sour milk; vegetarianism is the only road to
salvation of some, others insist not only on
vegetables alone, but on eating those raw . . .
The scientific truth may be put quite briefly:
eat moderately, having an ordinary
mixed diet, and don't worry.

Robert Hutchison, 1871-1960
British medical writer

The preservation of health is a duty.
Few seem conscious that there is such
a thing as physical morality.

Herbert Spencer, 1820-1903
English philosopher and journalist

Health is Wealth.
Look after it.

Sai Baba
Indian spiritual master

Heart

If a good face is a letter of recommendation, a
good heart is a letter of credit.

Edward Bulwer-Lytton, 1803-1873
English novelist, dramatist and politician

The heart's affections are divided like the
branches of the cedar tree; if the tree loses one
strong branch, it will suffer but it does not die.
It will pour all its vitality into the next branch
so that it will grow and fill the empty space.

Kahlil Gibran, 1883-1931
Lebanese poet, artist and mystic

There is no better exercise for the heart than
reaching down and lifting people up.

Anonymous

To put the world in order we must first put
the nation in order;
to put the nation in order, we must first put
the family in order;
to put the family in order, we must cultivate
our personal life;
and to cultivate our personal life, we must
set our hearts right.

Confucius, c. 550- c. 478 BC
Chinese philosopher

And now here is my secret, a very simple
secret; it is only with the heart that one
can see properly; what is essential is
invisible to the eye.

Antoine de Saint-Exupery, 1900-1944
French novelist and aviator

Heaven

My idea of heaven is eating foie gras to the
sound of trumpets.

Sydney Smith, 1771-1845
English clergyman, essayist and wit

Grant me paradise in this world; I'm not so
sure I'll reach it in the next.

Tintoretto, 1518-1594
Venetian painter

The loves that meet in Paradise shall
cast out fear,
And Paradise hath room for you and
me and all.

Christina Rossetti, 1830-1894
English poet

All we know
Of what they do above,
Is that they happy are, and that they love.

Edmund Waller, 1606-1687
English poet and politician

Helping

It is one of the most beautiful compensations of this life that no man can sincerely try to help another without helping himself.

Ralph Waldo Emerson, 1803-1882
American essayist, poet and philosopher

Doing nothing for others is the undoing of one's self. We must be purposely kind and generous or we miss the best part of life's existence. The heart that goes out of itself gets large and full of joy. This is the great secret of the inner life. We do ourselves most good by doing something for others.

Horace Mann, 1796-1859
American educationalist, writer and politician

If someone listens, or stretches out a hand, or whispers a word of encouragement, or attempts to understand a lonely person, extraordinary things begin to happen.

Loretta Girzatis, b. 1920
American educator and writer

Hands that help are holier than lips that pray.

Sai Baba
Indian spiritual master

When you tell your trouble to your neighbour you present him with a part of your heart. If he possesses a great soul, he thanks you; if he possesses a small one, he belittles you.

Kahlil Gibran, 1883-1931
Lebanese poet, artist and mystic

Do something for somebody every day for which you do not get paid.

Albert Schweitzer, 1875-1965
French medical missionary

No man can live happily who regards himself alone, who turns everything to his own advantage. Thou must live for another, if thou wishest to live for thyself.

Seneca, c. 4 BC - 65 AD
Roman philosopher, dramatist, poet and statesman

He who does not live in some degree for others, hardly lives for himself.

Michel de Montaigne, 1533-1592
French essayist

Only a life lived in the service of others is worth living.

Albert Einstein, 1879-1955
German-born American physicist

Home

He is happiest, be he king or peasant, who finds peace in his home.

Johann von Goethe, 1749-1832
German writer, dramatist and scientist

The ornament of a house is the friends who frequent it.

Ralph Waldo Emerson, 1803-1882
American essayist, poet and philosopher

The ideal of happiness has always taken material form in the house, whether cottage or castle; it stands for permanence and separation from the world.

Simone de Beauvoir, 1908-1986
French novelist

Seek home for rest,
For home is best.

Thomas Tusser, 1524-1580
English farmer

If you want a golden rule that will fit everybody, this is it. Have nothing in your houses that you do not know to be useful or believe to be beautiful.

William Morris, 1834-1896
English designer and craftsman

'Home' is any four walls that enclose the right person.

Helen Rowland, 1875-1950
American writer

Mid pleasures and palaces we may roam,
Be it ever so humble, there's no place
like home.

J. H. Payne, 1791-1852
American dramatist, poet and actor

The strength of a nation is derived from the
integrity of its homes.

Confucius, c. 551- c. 478 BC
Chinese philosopher

Hope

The frailest hope is better than despair.

Maria Brooks, 1795-1845
American poet

Of all the forces that make for a better world,
none is so indispensable, none so powerful as
hope. Without hope man is only half alive.

Charles Sawyer, 1887-1979
Writer

We judge of man's wisdom by his hope.

Ralph Waldo Emerson, 1803-1882
American essayist, poet and philosopher

Hope for the best, but prepare for the worst.

Proverb

Hope! of all ills that men endure
The only cheap and universal cure.

Abraham Cowley, 1618-1667
English poet and dramatist

He who has health has hope. And he who has
hope has everything.

Arabian proverb

Humour

Imagination was given to man to compensate for what he is not, and a sense of humour to console him for what he is.

Anonymous

A sense of humour is a sense of proportion.

Kahlil Gibran, 1883-1931
Lebanese poet, artist and mystic

The best sense of humour belongs to the man who can laugh at himself.

Anonymous

Our five senses are incomplete without the sixth — a sense of humour.

Anonymous

I

Ideals & Idealism

What is the use of living if it not be to strive
for noble causes and to make this muddled
world a better place for those who will live in
it after we are gone?

Winston Churchill, 1874-1965
British statesman and Prime Minister

The ideals that have lighted my way and, time
after time, have given me new courage to face
life cheerfully have been Kindness, Beauty and
Truth.

Albert Einstein, 1879-1955
German-born American physicist

Each time a man stands up for an ideal, or acts to improve the lot of others, or strikes out against injustice, he sends forth a tiny ripple of hope . . . and crossing each other from a million different centres of energy and daring those ripples build a current that can sweep down the mightiest walls of oppression and resistance.

Robert F. Kennedy, 1925-1968
American lawyer and politician

What do we live for, if it is not to make life less difficult for each other?

George Eliot (Mary Ann Evans), 1819-1880
English novelist

An ideal is often but a flaming vision of reality.

Joseph Conrad, 1857-1924
Polish-born English writer

Ideas

The ideas I stand for are not mine. I borrowed them from Socrates. I swiped them from Chesterfield. I stole them from Jesus. And I put them in a book. If you don't like their rules, whose would you use?

Dale Carnegie, 1888-1955
American writer and lecturer

Ideas shape the course of history.

John Maynard Keynes, 1883-1946
English economist

There's an element of truth in every idea that lasts long enough to be called corny.

Irving Berlin, 1888-1998
American composer

There is nothing in the world more powerful than an idea. No weapon can destroy it; no power can conquer it, except the power of another idea.

Anonymous

If you are possessed of an idea, you find it expressed everywhere, you even smell it.

Thomas Mann, 1875-1955
German writer

A belief is not merely an idea the mind possesses, it is an idea that possesses the mind.

Robert Bolton
English film director

Imagination

Knowledge is limited. Imagination encircles the whole world.

Albert Einstein, 1879-1955
German-born American physicist

Imagination is the beginning of creation. You imagine what you desire, you will what you imagine and at last you create what you will.

George Bernard Shaw, 1856-1950
Irish dramatist, writer and critic

Imagination finds a road to the realm of the gods, and there man can glimpse that which is to be after the soul's liberation from the world of substance.

Kahlil Gibran, 1883-1931
Lebanese poet, artist and mystic

When I examine myself and my methods of thought, I come to the conclusion that the gift of fantasy has meant more to me than my talent for absorbing positive knowledge.

Albert Einstein, 1879-1955
German-born American physicist

Imagination is the eye of the soul.

Jospeph Joubert, 1754-1824
French writer and moralist

Imperfection

All things are literally better, lovelier and more beloved for the imperfections which have been divinely appointed, that the law of human life may be Effort, and the law of human judgement — Mercy.

John Ruskin, 1819-1900
English author and art critic

Independence

The greatest thing in the world is to know how to be self-sufficient.

Michel de Montaigne, 1533-1592
French essayist

Individuality & Conformity

Every individual human being born on this earth has the capacity to become a unique and special person, unlike any who has ever existed before or will ever exist again.

Elisabeth Kübler-Ross, b. 1926
American psychiatrist and writer

Never be afraid to tread the path alone. Know which is your path and follow it wherever it may lead you; do not feel you have to follow in someone else's footsteps.

Eileen Caddy
Co-founder of the Findhorn Foundation, Scotland

Remember always that you have not only the right to be an individual, you have an obligation to be one. You cannot make any useful contribution in life unless you do this.

Eleanor Roosevelt, 1884-1962
First Lady of the United States of America, writer and diplomat

When she stopped conforming to the conventional picture of femininity she finally began to enjoy being a woman.

Betty Friedan, b. 1921
American feminist writer

It is a blessed thing that in every age someone has had the individuality enough and the courage enough to stand by his own convictions.

Robert G. Ingersoll, 1833-1899
American lawyer, politician and writer

Don't surrender your individuality, which is your greatest agent of power, to the customs and conventionalities that have got their life from the great mass . . . Do you want to be a power in the world? Then be yourself.

Ralph Waldo Trine, 1866-1958
American poet and writer

The best things and best people rise out of their separateness; I'm against a homogenised society because I want the cream to rise.

Robert Frost, 1874-1963
American poet

Once conform, once do what other people do because they do it, and a lethargy steals over all the finer nerves and faculties of the soul. She becomes all outer show and inner emptiness: dull, callous and indifferent.

Virginia Woolf, 1882-1941
English novelist

I am still puzzled as to how far the individual counts; a lot, I fancy, if he pushes the right way.

T. E. Lawrence (Lawrence of Arabia) 1888-1935
British soldier, archaeologist and author

What's a man's first duty?
The answer's brief: to be himself.

Henrik Ibsen, 1828-1906
Norwegian writer, dramatist and poet

I didn't belong as a kid, and that always bothered me. If only I'd known that one day my differentness would be an asset, then my early life would have been much easier.

Bette Midler, b. 1945
American singer and comedian

What is right for one soul may not be right for another. It may mean having to stand on your own and do something strange in the eyes of others. But do not be daunted. Do whatever it is because you know within it is right for you.

Eileen Caddy
Co-founder of the Findhorn Foundation, Scotland

At bottom every man knows well enough that he is a unique human being, only once on this earth: and by no extraordinary chance will such a marvellously picturesque piece of diversity in unity as he is, ever be put together a second time.

Friedrich Nietzsche, 1844-1900
German philosopher

Insight

A moment's insight is sometimes
worth a life's experience.

Oliver Wendell Holmes, 1809-1894
American writer and physician

Ideas often flit across our minds more
complete than we could make them after
much labour.

Duc de la Rochefoucauld, 1613-1680
French writer

In luminous flashes of sudden vision, we may
discover jewels of wisdom hidden within
ourselves. These flashes might come in words
(a powerful phrase or poem) or in a glowing
visual image or both. When these insights
reveal themselves to us, it is as if a veil of
mist simply dropped away. Universal and
timeless truths seem to emerge from the
shadows and stand bathed in the light of
deep understanding.

Lucia Capacchione
American art therapist

Intuition

Because of their age-long training in human relations — for that is what feminine intuition really is — women have a special contribution to make to any group enterprise . . .

Margaret Mead, 1901-1978
American anthropologist and writer

Invention

To invent, you need a good imagination and a pile of junk.

Thomas Edison, 1847-1931
American inventor

Invention is a combination of brains and materials. The more brains you use, the less materials you need.

Charles F. Kettering, 1876-1958
American engineer and inventor

J

Joy

Great joy, especially after a sudden change of circumstances, is apt to be silent, and dwells rather in the heart than on the tongue.

Henry Fielding, 1707-1754
English dramatist and writer

To get the full value of joy you must have someone to divide it with.

Mark Twain, 1835-1910
American humorist and writer

Joy seems to me a step beyond happiness — happiness is a sort of atmosphere you can live in sometimes when you're lucky. Joy is a light that fills you with hope and faith and love.

Adela Rogers St John, 1894-1988
American journalist

'On with the dance! Let joy be unconfined' is my motto, whether there's any dance to dance or joy to unconfine.

Mark Twain, 1835-1910
American humorist and writer

Man only likes to count his troubles, but he does not count his joys.

Feodor Dostoevsky, 1821-1881
Russian writer

There is no such thing as the pursuit of happiness, there is only the discovery of joy.

Joyce Grenfell, 1910-1979
English actress and writer

Judgement

There is so much good in the worst of us,
And so much bad in the best of us,
That it hardly becomes any of us
To talk about the rest of us.

Anonymous

Judge a tree from its fruit: not from the leaves.

Euripides, c. 484-406 BC
Greek dramatist and poet

Why beholdest thou the mote that is in thy
brother's eye, but considerest not the beam
that is in thy own eye?

Matthew, 7:3

No man can justly censure or condemn
another, because indeed no man truly
knows another.

Thomas Browne, 1605-1682
English physician and writer

Justice

Live and let live is the rule of common justice.

Sir Roger L'Estrange, 1616-1704
French writer

Injustice anywhere is a threat to
justice everywhere.

Martin Luther King, Jr, 1929-1968
American civil rights leader and minister

The probability that we may fail in the struggle
ought not to deter us from the support of a
cause we believe to be just.

Abraham Lincoln, 1809-1865
American statesman and President

K

Kindness

Guard within yourself that treasure, kindness.
Know how to give without hesitation, how to
lose without regret, how to acquire without
meanness . . . Know how to replace in your
heart, by the happiness of those you love, the
happiness that may be wanting in yourself.

George Sand (Amandine Dupin) 1804-1876
French novelist

Perfect kindness acts without
thinking of kindness.

Lao-Tze, c. 600 BC
Chinese philosopher and founder of Taoism

Your own soul is nourished when you are kind;
it is destroyed when you are cruel.

Proverbs 11: 17

Wise sayings often fall on barren ground; but a kind word is never thrown away.

Arthur Helps, 1813-1875
English historian

When you are kind to someone in trouble, you hope they'll remember and be kind to someone else. And it'll become like a wildfire.

Whoopi Goldberg, b. 1955
American actress

So many gods, so many creeds,
So many paths that wind and wind
While just the art of being kind
Is all the sad world needs.

Ella Wheeler Wilcox, 1850-1919
American writer and poet

A good deed is never lost. He who sows courtesy reaps friendship, and he who plants kindness gathers love.

Anonymous

Knowledge

Knowledge is power itself.

Francis Bacon, 1561-1626
British philosopher, essayist and courtier

Knowledge is of two kinds. We know a subject
ourselves, or we know where we can find
information upon it.

Samuel Johnson, 1709-1784
English lexicographer, essayist and wit

Knowledge and understanding are life's
faithful companions who will never be
untrue to you. For knowledge is your
crown, and understanding your staff; and
when they are with you, you can possess
no greater treasures.

Kahlil Gibran, 1883-1931
Lebanese poet, artist and mystic

If we value the pursuit of knowledge we must be free to follow wherever that search may lead us.

Adlai Stevenson, 1900-1965
American lawyer, statesman and
United Nations representative

A man's merit lies in his knowledge and deeds, not in his colour, faith, race or descent. For remember, my friend, the son of a shepherd who possesses knowledge is of greater worth to a nation than the heir to the throne, if he be ignorant. Knowledge is your true patent of nobility, no matter who your father or what your race may be.

Kahlil Gibran, 1883-1931
Lebanese poet, artist and mystic

The desire of knowledge, like the thirst of riches, increases ever with the acquisition of it.

Laurence Sterne, 1713-1768
British writer and clergyman

L

Laughter

Let there be more joy and laughter
in your living.

Eileen Caddy
Co-founder of the Findhorn Foundation, Scotland

You grow up the day you have your first real
laugh at yourself.

Ethel Barrymore, 1879-1959
American actress

Laughter gives us distance. It allows us
to step back from an event, deal with
it, and then move on.

Bob Newhart
American comedian

Laughter is a property in man
essential to his reason.

Lewis Carroll, 1832-1898
English writer, mathematician and clergyman

It is a splendid habit to laugh inwardly at
yourself. It is the best way of regaining your
good humour and of finding God without
further anxiety.

Abbé de Tourville, 1842-1903
French priest

The two best physicians of them all —
Dr Laughter and Dr Sleep.

Gregory Dean, 1907-1979
British physician

Laughter can relieve tension, soothe the pain of
disappointment, and strengthen the spirit for
the formidable tasks that always lie ahead.

Dwight D. Eisenhower, 1890-1969
American statesman and President

If you like a man's laugh before you know anything of him, you may say with confidence that he is a good man.

Feodor Dostoevsky, 1821-1881
Russian writer

When you know how to laugh and when to look upon things as too absurd to take seriously, the other person is ashamed to carry through even if he was serious about it.

Eleanor Roosevelt, 1884-1962
First Lady of the United States of America, writer and diplomat

A man isn't really poor if he can still laugh.

Anonymous

Leadership

Setting an example is not the main means of influencing another, it is the only means.

Albert Einstein, 1879-1955
German-born American physicist

The question, 'Who ought to be boss?' is like asking 'Who ought to be the tenor in the quartet?' Obviously, the man who can sing tenor.

Henry Ford, 1863-1947
American car manufacturer

Treat people as if they were what they ought to be, and you help them become what they are capable of becoming.

Johann von Goethe, 1749-1832
German writer, dramatist and scientist

Our chief want is someone who will inspire us to be what we know we could be.

Ralph Waldo Emerson, 1803-1882
American essayist, poet and philosopher

Leisure

Work is not always required . . . there is such a
thing as sacred idleness, the cultivation of
which is now fearfully neglected.

George MacDonald, 1824-1905
British poet

It is impossible to enjoy idling thoroughly
unless one has plenty of work to do.

Jerome K. Jerome, 1859-1927
English humorous writer and novelist

To be able to fill leisure intelligently is the last
product of civilisation.

Bertrand Russell, 1872-1970
English philosopher, mathematician and writer

A perpetual holiday is a good working
definition of hell.

George Bernard Shaw, 1856-1950
Irish dramatist, writer and critic

Life

As long as you live, keep learning how to live.

Seneca, c. 4 BC-65 AD
Roman dramatist, poet and statesman

Is it so small a thing
To have enjoy'd the sun,
To have liv'd light
In the spring,
To have lov'd, to have thought, to have done?

Matthew Arnold, 1822-1888
English poet, essayist and educationalist

I could not, at any age, be content to take my place in a corner by the fireside and simply look on. Life was meant to be lived. Curiosity must be kept alive. The fatal thing is the rejection. One must never, for whatever reason, turn his back on life.

Eleanor Roosevelt, 1884-1962
First Lady of the United States of America, writer and diplomat

Life is a single short sentence — but I want my life to read like a beautiful sentence, one that nobody wants to end.

Neil Diamond
American singer/songwriter

Do not take life too seriously. You will never get out of it alive.

Elbert Hubbard, 1856-1915
American writer

My feeling about life is a curious kind of triumphant sensation about seeing it bleak, knowing it so, and walking into it fearlessly because one has no choice.

Georgia O'Keefe, 1887-1986
American artist

Try as much as possible to be wholly alive, with all your might, and when you laugh, laugh like hell, and when you get angry, get good and angry. Try to be alive because you will be dead soon enough.

William Saroyan, 1908-1981
American writer and dramatist

There is no cure for birth and death, save to enjoy the interval.

George Santayana, 1863-1952
Spanish philosopher and writer

It's not how things turn out — it's the joy of doing it!

Barbra Streisand, b. 1942
American singer and actress

Let your life lightly dance on the edges of Time like dew on the tip of a leaf.

Rabindranath Tagore, 1861-1941
Indian poet and philosopher

Life is good only when it is magical and musical, a perfect timing and consent, and when we do not anatomise it. You must treat the days respectfully . . . You must hear the bird's song without attempting to render it into nouns and verbs.

Ralph Waldo Emerson, 1803-1882
American essayist, poet and philosopher

The love of life is necessary to the vigorous prosecution of any undertaking.

Samuel Johnson, 1709-1784
English lexicographer, essayist and wit

The purpose of life is to matter — to count, to stand for something, to have it make some difference that we lived at all.

Leo Rosten, b. 1908
Polish-born American writer and humorist

There are two things to aim for in life: first to get what you want; and, after that, to enjoy it. Only the wisest of mankind achieve the second.

Logan Pearsall Smith, 1865-1946
American-born British wit, writer and critic

Life is a traveller on a Holy journey.

Sai Baba
Indian spiritual master

The bread of life is love, the salt of love is work, the sweetness of life is poetry, and the water of life is faith.

Anna Jameson, 1794-1860
English writer

Life is no brief candle to me, it is a sort of splendid torch which I've got hold of for the moment and I want to make it burn as bright as possible before handing it on to a future generation.

George Bernard Shaw, 1856-1950
Irish dramatist, writer and critic

At the end of your life, you will never regret not having passed one more test, not winning one more verdict or not closing one more deal. You will regret time not spent with a husband, a friend, a child or parent.

Barbara Bush, b. 1925
First Lady of the United States of America

I have never given very deep thought to a philosophy of life, though I have a few ideas that I think are very useful to me:

Do whatever comes your way to do as well as you can.
Think as little as possible about yourself.
Think as much as possible about other people.
Dwell on things that are interesting.
Since you get more joy out of giving joy to others you should put a good deal of thought into the happiness that you are able to give.

Eleanor Roosevelt, 1884-1962
First Lady of the United States of America, writer and diplomat

The most fruitful of all the arts is the art of living well.

Cicero, 106-43 BC
Roman orator

Loneliness

Always remember that you are not the only one who has ever felt rejected, unloved and lonely at some time. Reach out and help someone else in trouble, and you could be amazed at the changes in yourself — and your life!

Anonymous

If you want people to be glad to meet you, you must be glad to meet them — and show it.

Johann von Goethe, 1749-1832
German writer, dramatist and scientist

Loneliness is a state of mind.

Anonymous

Love

Great is the power of might and mind,
But only love can make us kind,
And all we are or hope to be
Is empty pride and vanity —
If love is not a part of all
The greatest man is very small.

Helen Steiner Rice, 1900-1981
American poet

The story of love is not important —
what is important is that one is capable of love.
It is perhaps the only glimpse we are permitted
of eternity.

Helen Hayes, 1900-1993
American actress

If we make our goal to live a life of
compassion and unconditional love, then the
world will indeed become a garden where all
kinds of flowers can bloom and grow.

Elisabeth Kübler-Ross, b. 1926
Swiss-born American psychiatrist and writer

Love is patient, love is kind. It does not envy, it does not boast, it is not proud. It is not rude, it is not self-seeking, it is not easily angered, it keeps no records of wrongs . . .

1 Corinthians 13: 4-5

Ego wants to get and forget,
Love want to give and forgive.

Sai Baba
Indian spiritual master

Above all, love each other deeply, because love covers over a multitude of sins.

Peter 4:8

There is a land of the living and a land of the dead, and the bridge is love.

Thornton Wilder, 1897-1975
American author and dramatist

Love begins when a person feels another person's need to be as important as his own.

Anonymous

Love makes all hard hearts gentle.

George Herbert, 1593-1633
English poet

Love is the only force capable of transforming
an enemy into a friend.

Martin Luther King, Jr, 1929-1968
American civil rights leader and minister

In our life there is a single colour, as on an
artist's palette, which provides the meaning of
life and art. It is the colour of love.

Marc Chagall, 1887-1985
French artist

Immature love says: 'I love you
because I need you.'
Mature love says: 'I need you
because I love you.'

Erich Fromm, 1900-1980
American psychoanalyst

One word frees us of all the weight and pain of life; that word is love.

Sophocles, 496-406 BC
Greek tragedian

All love is sweet,
Given or returned
Common as light is love,
And its familiar voice wearies not ever.

Percy Bysshe Shelley, 1792-1822
English poet

A loving heart is the truest wisdom.

Charles Dickens, 1812-1870
English writer

Love will teach us all things: but we must learn how to win love; it is got with difficulty: it is a possession dearly bought with much labour and a long time; for one must love not sometimes only, for a passing moment, but always. And let not men's sin dishearten thee: love a man even in his sin, for that love is a likeness of the divine love, and is the summit of love on earth.

Feodor Dostoevsky, 1821-1881
Russian novelist

Love is a fruit in season at all times, and within reach of every hand.

Mother Teresa of Calcutta, 1910-1997
Yugoslav-born missionary

To love another person is to help them love God.

Soren Kierkegaard, 1813-1855
Danish philosopher and theologian

Love comforteth like sunshine after rain.

William Shakespeare, 1564-1616
English playwright and poet

The root of the matter is a very simple and old-fashioned thing, a thing so simple that I am almost ashamed to mention it for fear of the derisive smile with which wise cynics will greet my words. The thing I mean — please forgive me for mentioning it — is love, or compassion. If you feel this, you have a motive for existence, a guide in action, a reason for courage, an imperative necessity for intellectual honesty.

Bertrand Russell, 1872-1970
English philosopher, mathematician and writer

Luck

The harder you work, the luckier you get.

Gary Player, b. 1935
South African golfer

Luck is being ready for the chance.

Anonymous

I never knew an early-rising, hard-working,
prudent man, careful of his earnings, and
strictly honest, who complained of bad luck.

Joseph Addison, 1672-1719
English essayist and politician

Luck is infatuated with the efficient.

Persian proverb

Good luck often has the odour of perspiration
about it.

Anonymous

Shallow men believe in luck. Strong men believe in cause and effect.

Ralph Waldo Emerson, 1803-1882
American essayist, poet and philosopher

Luck is good planning, carefully executed.

Anonymous

Good luck is what a lazy man calls a hard-working man's success.

Anonymous

M

Marriage

A marriage makes of two fractional lines a
whole; it give to two purposeless lives a work,
and doubles the strength of each to perform it;
it gives to two questioning natures a reason for
living and something to live for.

Mark Twain, 1835-1910
American humorist and writer

The most important things to do in this world
are to get something to eat, something to drink
and somebody to love you.

Brendan Behan, 1923-1964
Irish writer

Love one another, but make not a bond
of love;

Let it rather be a moving sea between the
shores of your souls.
Fill each other's cup but drink not from the
one cup.
Give one another of your bread but eat not
from the same loaf.
Sing and dance together and be joyous, but
let each one of you be alone.
Even as the strings of a lute are alone
though they quiver with the same music.

Kahlil Gibran, 1883-1931
Lebanese poet, artist and mystic

A good marriage is like Dr Who's Tardis, small
and banal from the outside but spacious and
interesting from within.

Katharine Whitehorn, b. 1938
English essayist and politician

Well, what is a relationship? It's about two people having tremendous weaknesses and vulnerabilities, like we all do, and one person being able to strengthen the other in their areas of vulnerability. And vice versa. You need each other. You complete each other, passion and romance aside.

Jane Fonda, b. 1937
American actor and political activist

Love thy wife as thyself; honour her more than thyself. He who lives unmarried lives without joy . . . The children of a man who marries for money will prove a curse to him. All the blessings of a household come through the wife, therefore should her husband honour her.

The Talmud

Partnership, not dependence, is the real romance in marriage.

Muriel Fox, b. 1928
American business executive

She who dwells with me,
Whom I loved with such communion,
That no place on earth
Can ever be a solitude to me.

William Blake, 1710-1850
English poet

Men and women are made to love each other.
It's only by loving each other that they can
achieve anything.

Christina Stead, 1902-1983
Australian novelist

Let not the marriage of true minds
Admit impediments. Love is not love
Which alters when it alterations finds,
Or bends with the remover to remove.

William Shakespeare, 1564-1616
English dramatist and poet

How do I love thee? Let me count the ways.
I love thee to the depth and breadth and
height my soul can reach.

Elizabeth Barrett Browning, 1806-1861
English poet

Mind

The mind is an iceberg — it floats with only one-seventh of its bulk above water.

Sigmund Freud, 1856-1939
Austrian founder of psychoanalysis

The true, strong and sound mind is the mind that can embrace equally great things and small.

Samuel Johnson, 1709-1784
English lexicographer, essayist and wit

The mind ought sometimes to be amused, that it may the better return to thought and to itself.

Phaedrus, c. 15 BC-50 AD
Translator of Aesop's fables into Latin

Miracles

Miracles are instantaneous; they cannot be summoned but they come of themselves, usually at unlikely moments and to those who least expect them.

Katherine A. Porter, 1890-1980
American author

Miracles happen only to those who believe in them. Otherwise why does not the Virgin Mary appear to Lamaists, Mohammedans or Hindus, who have never heard of her?

Bernard Berenson, 1865-1959
American art critic

There are two ways to live your life. One is as though nothing is a miracle. The other is as though everything is a miracle.

Albert Einstein, 1879-1955
German-born American physicist

Mistakes

You know, by the time you've reached my age, you've made plenty of mistakes if you've lived your life properly.

Ronald Reagan, b. 1911
President of the United States of America

Anyone who has never made a mistake has never tried anything new.

Albert Einstein, 1879-1955
German-born American physicist

Nobody makes a greater mistake than he who does nothing because he could do so litttle.

Edmund Burke, 1729-1797
British politician

Even a mistake may turn out to be the one thing necessary to a worthwhile achievement.

Henry Ford, 1863-1947
American car manufacturer

Morality

What is moral is what you feel good after, and what is immoral is what you feel bad after.

Ernest Hemingway, 1899-1964
American novelist

If your morals make you dreary, depend upon it, they are wrong.

Robert Louis Stevenson, 1850-1894
Scottish writer

Music

Music produces a kind of pleasure which human nature cannot do without.

Confucius, c. 550-c. 478BC
Chinese philosopher

Music has charms to soothe a savage breast.

William Congreve, 1670-1729
British dramatist

After silence, that which comes closer to
expressing the inexpressible is music.

Aldous Huxley, 1894-1963
English writer

Music religious hearts inspires;
It wakes the soul, and lifts it high,
And wings it with sublime desires,
And fits it to bespeak the Deity.

Joseph Addison, 1672-1719
English essayist

Mozart's music gives us permission to live.

John Updike, b. 1932
American novelist and poet

N

Nature

Come forth into the light of things,
Let Nature be your teacher.

William Wordsworth, 1770-1850
British poet

After you have exhausted what there is in
business, politics, conviviality, and so on —
have found that none of these finally satisfy,
or permanently wear — what remains?
Nature remains.

Walt Whitman, 1819-1892
American poet

Nature never did betray
The heart that loved her.

William Wordsworth, 1770-1850
British poet

Tune your ear
To all the wordless music of the stars
And to the voice of nature, and your heart
Shall turn to truth and goodness as the plant
Turns to the sun . . .

Ralph Waldo Trine, 1866-1958
American poet and writer

Love all God's creation, both the whole and every grain of sand. Love every leaf, every ray of light. Love the animals, love the plants, love each separate thing. If thou love each thing thou wilt perceive the mystery of God in all; and when once thou perceive this, thou wilt thenceforth grow every day to a fuller understanding of it: until thou come at last to love the whole world with a love that will then be all-embracing and universal.

Feodor Dostoevsky, 1821-1881
Russian novelist

There is a pleasure in the pathless woods,
There is a rapture on the lonely shore,
There is society, where none intrudes,
By the deep Sea, and music in its roar:
I love not Man the less, but Nature more.

Lord Byron, 1788-1824
English poet

To see a world in a Grain of Sand,
And a Heaven in a Wild Flower,
Hold Infinity in the palm of your hand,
And Eternity in an hour.

William Blake, 1757-1827
English poet and artist

Those undescribed, ambrosial mornings when a
thousand birds were heard gently twittering
and ushering in the light, like the argument to
a new canto of an epic and heroic poem. The
serenity, the infinite promise of such a morning
...Then there was something divine and
immortal in our life.

Henry David Thoreau, 1817-1862
American essayist, poet and mystic

Pity the eye that sees no more in the sun than a stove to keep it warm and a torch to light its way between the home and business office. That is a blind eye, even if capable of seeing a fly a mile away.

Kahlil Gibran, 1883-1931
Lebanese poet, artist and mystic

All through my life, the new sights of Nature made me rejoice like a child.

Marie Curie, 1867-1934
Polish-born chemist

Every morning was a cheerful invitation to make my life of equal simplicity, and I may say innocence, with Nature herself.

Henry David Thoreau, 1817-1862
American essayist, poet and mystic

O

Obstacles

Obstacles are those frightful things you see
when you take your eyes off your goal.

Henry Ford, 1863-1947
American car manufacturer

Opportunity

All of us do not have equal talent, but all of us
should have an equal opportunity to develop
our talents.

John F. Kennedy, 1917-1963
President of the United States of America

There is no security on this earth; there is only
opportunity.

General Douglas MacArthur, 1880-1964
American military leader

God helps those that help themselves.

Benjamin Franklin, 1706-1790
American statesman and scientist

Grab a chance and you won't be sorry for a
might-have-been.

Arthur Ransome, 1844-1967
British novelist

There is a tide in the affairs of men
Which, taken at the flood, leads on to
    fortune;
Omitted, all the voyage of their life
Is bound in shallows and in miseries.
On such a full sea are we now afloat,
And we must take the current when it
    serves,
Or lose our ventures.

William Shakespeare, 1564-1616
English poet and playwright

When one door closes, another opens; but
often we look so long at the closed door that
we do not see the one that has opened.

Anonymous

Next to knowing when to seize an opportunity, the most important thing in life is to know when to forgo an advantage.

Benjamin Disraeli, 1804-1881
British Prime Minister and writer

Great opportunities come to men who make the most of small ones.

Anonymous

Optimism

I am an optimist. It does not seem too much use being anything else.

Winston Churchill, 1874-1965
British statesman, Prime Minister and writer

One of the things I learned the hard way was that it doesn't pay to get discouraged. Keeping busy and making optimism a way of life can restore your faith in yourself.

Lucille Ball, 1911-1989
American actress

It's easy to become disheartened by the constant stream of tragedy and violence that is beamed into our living rooms, but never lose sight of the fact that many dedicated individuals and organisations are working constantly to ameliorate suffering. So next time it all seems too much to bear, focus on all the good being done by these good people.

Anonymous

All things are possible until they are proved impossible — even the impossible may only be so, as of now.

Pearl S. Buck, 1892-1972
American writer and missionary

Make the most of the best and the least of the worst.

Robert Louis Stevenson, 1850-1894
Scottish writer and poet

There is not enough darkness in the whole world to extinguish the light of one small candle.

Spanish proverb

I am an optimist, unrepentant and militant.
After all, in order not to be a fool an optimist
must know how sad a place the world
can be. It is only the pessimist who finds
this out anew every day.

Peter Ustinov b. 1921
English writer, actor and dramatist

A positive thinker does not refuse to *recognise*
the negative, he refuses to *dwell* on it. Positive
thinking is a form of thought which habitually
looks for the best results from the worst
conditions. It is possible to look for something
to build on; it is possible to expect the best for
yourself even though things look bad. And the
remarkable fact is that when you seek good,
you are very likely to find it.

Norman Vincent Peale, 1898-1993
American writer and minister

The optimist is wrong as often as is the
pessimist. But he has a lot more fun.

Anonymous

Inside my head I construct an airtight box. I keep inside it what I want to think about and everything else stays beyond the walls. . . Inside is love and friends and optimism. Outside is negativity, can't do-ism, any criticism of me and mine. Most of the time the box is as strong as steel.

Virginia Kelley
Mother of President Clinton

However much I am at the mercy of the world, I never let myself get lost by brooding over its misery. I hold firmly to the thought that each one of us can do a little to bring some portion of that misery to an end.

Albert Schweitzer, 1875-1965
French medical missionary

'Tis easy enough to be pleasant,
When life flows along like a song;
But the man worthwhile is the one
    who will smile
When everything goes dead wrong.

Ella Wheeler Wilcox, 1850-1919
American writer and poet

Two men look out between the same bars:
One sees mud, and one the stars.

Frederick Langbridge, 1849-1923
Irish religious writer

A good business manager hires optimists for the sales department and pessimists for the accounts department.

Anonymous

The world is changing and it is my optimistic belief that gradually, patchily, maybe with one step back for every two steps forward, it is changing for the better.

Pamela Bone
Australian journalist

Originality

Every human being is intended to have a character of his own; to be what no others are, and to do what no other can do.

William Ellery Channing, 1780-1842
American clergyman

The merit of originality is not novelty; it is sincerity. The believing man is the original man; whatsoever he believes, he believes it for himself, not for another.

Thomas Carlyle, 1795-1881
Scottish historian, essayist and critic

Originality exists in every individual because each of us differs from the others. We are all primary numbers divisible only by ourselves.

Jean Guitton
French writer

P

Parting

When you part from your friend, you grieve
not; for that which you love most in him may
be clearer in his absence, as the mountain to
the climber is clearer from the plain.

Kahlil Gibran, 1883-1931
Lebanese poet, artist and mystic

Adieu, adieu, kind friends, adieu, adieu, adieu,
I can no longer stay with you, stay with you.
I'll hang my harp on a weeping willow-tree,
And may the world go well with thee.

Unknown

Peace

The world will never have lasting peace so long as men reserve for war the finest human qualities. Peace, no less than war, requires idealism and self-sacrifice and a righteous and dynamic faith.

John Foster Dulles, 1888-1959
American Secretary of State

I am a man of peace. I believe in peace. But I do not want peace at any price. I do not want the peace that you find in stone; I do not want the peace that you find in the grave; but I do want the peace which you find embedded in the human breast, which is exposed to the arrows of the world, but which is protected from all harm by the power of Almighty God.

Gandhi, 1869-1948
Indian political leader

Peace is a daily, a weekly, a monthly process, gradually changing opinions, slowly eroding old barriers, quietly building new structures. And however undramatic the pursuit of peace, the pursuit must go on.

John F. Kennedy, 1917-1963
President of the United States of America

The peace of God, the peace of men,
Be upon each window, each door,
Upon each hole that lets in light,
Upon the four corners of my house,
Upon the four corners of my bed.

Gaelic blessing

Peace is not an absence of war, it is a virtue, a state of mind, a disposition for benevolence, confidence, justice.

Benedict Spinoza, 1632-1677
Dutch philosopher

Perseverance

When you get into a tight place and everything
goes against you, till it seems as though you
could not hang on a minute longer, never give
up then, for that is just the place and time that
the tide will turn.

Harriet Beecher Stowe, 1811-1989
American author and social reformer

When I was a young man, I observed that
nine out of ten things I did were failures.
I didn't want to be a failure, so I did ten
times more work.

George Bernard Shaw, 1856-1950
Irish dramatist, writer and critic

Winners never quit — and quitters never win.

Anonymous

By perseverance the snail reached the ark.

Charles Haddon Spurgeon, 1834-1892
British Baptist preacher

I'm extraordinarily patient, provided I get my own way in the end.

Margaret Thatcher, b. 1925
British Prime Minister

We haven't failed. We now know a thousand things that won't work, so we're that much closer to finding what will.

Thomas Edison, 1847-1931
American inventor

Never give in! Never give in! Never, never never — in nothing great or small, large or petty — never give in except to convictions of honour and good sense.

Winston Churhill, 1874-1965
British statesman and Prime Minister

Great works are performed not by strength but by perseverance.

Samuel Johnson, 1709-1784
English lexicographer, essayist and wit

If at first you don't succeed,
Try, try again.

William Edward Hickson, 1803-1870
British educationalist

Too many people let others stand in their way
and don't go back for one more try.

Rosabeth Moss Kanter, b. 1943
American writer and educator

Austere perseverance, harsh and continuous,
may be employed by the smallest of us and
rarely fails its purpose, for its silent power
grows irresistibly greater with time.

Johann von Goethe, 1749-1832
German writer, dramatist and scientist

Pleasure

Pleasure is very seldom found where it is sought; our brightest blazes of gladness are commonly kindled by unexpected sparks.

Samuel Johnson, 1709-1784
English lexicographer, essayist and wit

Give me books, fruit, French wine and fine weather and a little music out of doors, played by someone I don't know.

John Keats, 1795-1821
British poet

A book of verses underneath the Bough,
A jug of Wine, a Loaf of Bread — and Thou
Beside me singing in the Wilderness;
O! Wilderness were Paradise enow!

Omar Khayyam, 1048-1131 AD
Persian poet

Potential

If we did all the things we are capable of doing
we would truly astound ourselves.

Thomas Edison, 1847-1931
American inventor

Compared to what we ought to be we are
only half awake. We are making use of only a
small part of our physical and mental
resources. Stating the thing broadly, the human
individual thus lives far within his limits.
He possesses the power of various sorts which
he habitually fails to use.

William James, 1842-1910
American psychologist and philosopher

No matter what your level of ability, you have
more potential than you can ever develop in a
lifetime.

Anonymous

Power

The sole advantage of power is that you can do more good.

Seneca c. 4 BC-65 AD
Roman philosopher, dramatist, poet and statesman

No extraordinary power should be lodged in any one individual.

Thomas Paine, 1737-1809
English-born American revolutionary, philosopher and writer

I have never been able to conceive how any rational being could propose happiness to himself from the exercise of power over others.

Thomas Jefferson, 1743-1826
President of the United States of America

Praise

If you don't like what I do, tell me. If you like what I do, tell my boss.

Sign on department store counter

There is no such whetstone, to sharpen a good wit and encourage a will to learning, as is praise.

Roger Ascham, 1515-1568
English scholar and educationalist

It is a sure sign of mediocrity to be niggardly with praise.

Marquis de Vauvenargues, 1715-1747
French soldier and moralist

Praise is the best diet for us, after all.

Sydney Smith, 1771-1845
English clergyman, essayist and wit

Man lives more by affirmation than by bread.

Victor Hugo, 1802-1885
French poet and writer

The advantage of doing one's praising for
oneself is that one can lay it on so thick and
exactly in the right places.

Samuel Butler, 1835-1902
English writer

The test of any man's character is how
he takes praise.

Anonymous

Prayer

Teach us to delight in simple things,
And mirth that has no bitter springs;
Forgiveness free of evil done,
And love to all men 'neath the sun.

Rudyard Kipling, 1865-1936
Indian-born British writer and poet

Who rises from Prayer a better man,
    his prayer is answered.

George Meredith, 1831-1891
English poet and statesman

Prayer is the song of the heart. It reaches the
ear of God even if it is mingled with the cry
and tumult of a thousand men.

Kahlil Gibran, 1883-1931
Lebanese poet, artist and mystic

Let me be a little kinder,
Let me be a little blinder
To the faults of those around me.

Edgar A. Guest, 1881-1959
English-born American journalist, poet and author

Prejudice

Prejudices, it is well known, are most difficult to eradicate from the heart whose soil has never been loosened or fertilised by education; they grow there, firm as weeds among rocks.

Charlotte Brontë, 1816-1855
British novelist

It is never too late to give up your prejudices.

Henry David Thoreau, 1817-1862
American essayist, poet and mystic

What white people have to do is to find out in their own hearts why it is necessary to have a nigger in the first place. I'm not a nigger, I am a man, but if you think I'm a nigger, it means you need to.

James Baldwin, 1924-1987
American writer, poet and civil rights activist

Most prejudice is based upon fear of the unknown.

Anonymous

Problems

If there was nothing wrong in the world, there wouldn't be anything for us to to do.

George Bernard Shaw, 1856-1950
Irish dramatist, writer and critic

Problems are a major part of life.
Don't whinge about why you always have problems. Rest assured, no matter what, throughout your life you will always have to deal with problems. So don't waste time.
Get on with the solving. Take it from someone who has been there — the solving gets easier as you go along.

Sara Henderson, b. 1936
Australian outback station manager and writer

A problem well stated is a problem half solved.

Charles Franklin Kettering, 1876-1958
American engineer and inventor

It is in the whole process of meeting and solving problems that life has meaning. Problems are the cutting edge that distinguishes between success and failure. Problems call forth our courage and our wisdom; indeed, they create our courage and our wisdom. It is only because of problems that we grow mentally and spiritually. It is through the pain of confronting and resolving problems that we learn.

M. Scott Peck, b. 1936
American psychiatrist and writer

I think these difficult times have helped me to understand better than before how infinitely rich and beautiful life is in every way and that so many things that one goes around worrying about are of no importance whatsoever.

Isak Dinesen (Karen Blixen) 1885-1962
Danish writer

Those things that hurt, instruct.

Benjamin Franklin, 1706-1790
American statesman and scientist

The marvellous richness of human experience would lose something of rewarding joy if there were no limitations to overcome. The hilltop hour would not be half so wonderful if there were no dark valleys to traverse.

Helen Keller, 1880-1968
Blind and deaf American writer and scholar

Remember, without that uncomfortable bit of grit, the oyster would not produce those priceless pearls.

Anonymous

When it is dark enough, you can see the stars.

Ralph Waldo Emerson, 1803-1882
American essayist, poet and philosopher

R

Regret

I don't regret anything I've ever done, so long as I enjoyed doing it at the time.

Katharine Hepburn, b. 1909
American actress

Make it a rule of life never to regret and never look back. We all live in suspense, from day to day, from hour to hour; in other words, we are the hero of our own story.

Mary McCarthy, 1912-1989
American author and critic

Regret is an appalling waste of energy; you can't build on it; it is good only for wallowing in.

Katherine Mansfield, 1888-1923
New Zealand short story writer

Be not like him who sits by his fireside and watches the fire go out, then blows vainly upon the dead ashes. Do not give up hope or yield to despair because of that which is past, for to bewail the irretrievable is the worst of human frailties.

Kahlil Gibran, 1883-1931
Lebanese poet, artist and mystic

I have no regrets. I wouldn't have lived my life the way I did if I was going to worry about what people were going to say.

Ingrid Bergman, 1915-1982
Swedish-born American actress

There's no point dwelling on what might or could have been. You just have to go forward.

Jack Nicholson, b. 1937
American actor

You can't have rosy views about the future if your mind is full of the blues about the past.

Anonymous

Relationships

You haven't learned life's lesson very well if you haven't noticed that you can give the tone or colour, or decide the reaction you want of people in advance. It's unbelievably simple.

If you want them to take an interest in you, take an interest in them first.

If you want to make them nervous, become nervous yourself.

If you want them to shout and raise their voices, raise yours and shout.

If you want them to strike you, strike first.

It's as simple as that. People will treat you as you treat them. It's no secret. Look about you. You can prove it with the next person you meet.

Winston Churchill, 1874-1965
British statesman and Prime Minister

The world is a looking glass, and gives back to every man the reflection of his own face.

William Makepeace Thackeray, 1811-1863
British writer

A man's feeling of good-will towards others is the strongest magnet for drawing good-will towards himself.

Lord Chesterfield, 1694-1773
English statesman

We can't choose our relatives or workmates. But if you find yourself forced to put up with the company of someone who really rubs you up the wrong way, try to find something about them that you like. Then focus on that quality. You'll feel better, and the other person may even respond to your more accepting attitude.

Anonymous

People is all everything is, all it has ever been, all it can ever be.

William Saroyan, 1908-1981
American writer and dramatist

Relaxation

Treat yourself to a massage, hire a favourite video, have a hot bath and an early night, or read a book in the sun — make a point of doing something really relaxing as often as you can. It will do you no end of good physically and mentally, and will re-charge your batteries so you can face up to life's everyday challenges.

Anonymous

Religion

I love you, my brother, whoever you are — whether you worship in your church, kneel in your temple, or pray in your mosque. You and I are all children of one faith, for the diverse paths of religion are fingers of the loving hand of one Supreme Being, a hand extended to all, offering completeness of spirit to all, eager to receive all.

Kahlil Gibran, 1881-1931
Lebanese poet, artist and mystic

One's religion is whatever one is most interested in.

J. M. Barrie, 1860-1937
Scottish writer and dramatist

I am a deeply religious unbeliever.

Albert Einstein, 1879-1955
German-born American physicist

It makes all the difference in the world to your life whether you arrive at a philosophy and a religion or not. It makes the difference between living in a world which is merely a constant changing mass of phenomena and living in a significant, ordered universe.

Mary Ellen Chase, 1887-1973
American educator and author

In my religion there would be no exclusive doctrine; all would be love, poetry and doubt.

Cyril Connolly, 1903-1974
English writer, critic and literary editor

Every religion is a Lamp that illumines
the Path of Truth.

Sai Baba
Indian spiritual master

The cosmic religious experience is the
strongest and noblest driving force behind
scientific research.

Albert Einstein, 1879-1955
German-born American physicist

Responsibility

The willingness to accept responsibilty for
one's own life is the source from which self-
respect springs.

Joan Didion, b. 1935
American writer and journalist

None of us is responsible for all the things that
happen to us, but we are responsible for the
way we react to them.

Anonymous

Restrictions

Every man takes the limits of his own vision
for the limits of the world.

Arthur Schopenhauer, 1788-1860
German philosopher

I think the very restrictions which were put
on woman, which made her emphasise the
personal world, caused something very good
to be born. Whereas men dealt in terms of
nations, in terms of statistics, abstract ideology,
woman, because her world was restricted to
the personal, was more human. Now that she
is beginning to step beyond her confines, I
hope she can bring to the world the sense of
personal value of human beings, some
empathy and some sympathy.

Anaïs Nin, 1909-1977
French writer

Right

We should always do right, because it will gratify some people and astonish the rest.

Mark Twain, 1835-1910
American humorist and writer

Risk

Take calculated risks. This is quite different from being rash.

George S. Patton, 1885-1945
American military leader

Being myself includes taking risks with myself, taking risks on new behaviour, trying new ways of 'being myself', so that I can see how it is I want to be.

Hugh Prather, b. 1938
American writer

To gain that which is worth having, it may be necessary to lose everything.

Bernadette Devlin, b. 1947
Irish politician

No man is worth his salt who is not ready at all times to risk his body, to risk his well-being, to risk his life in a great cause.

Theodore Roosevelt, 1858-1919
President of the United States of America

Courageous risks are life-giving. They help you grow, make you brave and better than you think you are.

Joan L. Curcio
American educator

S

Self-acceptance

I was raised to sense what someone wanted
me to be and to be that kind of person. It
took me a long time not to judge myself
through someone else's eyes.

Sally Field, b. 1946
American actor

I was born a jackdaw; why should I be an owl?

Ogden Nash, 1902-1971
American humorous poet

There are big dogs and little dogs, but the
little dogs should not be disheartened by the
existence of the big dogs. All must bark, and
bark with the voice God gave them.

Anton Chekhov, 1860-1904
Russian dramatist and short story writer

One has just to be oneself.
That's my basic message.
The moment you accept yourself as you are,
all burdens, all mountainous burdens,
simply disappear.
Then life is a sheer joy, a festival of lights.

Bhagwan Shree Rajneesh
Indian spiritual leader

Self-confidence

I'm trying to be myself more and more. The more confidence you have in yourself, which I think only comes with experience and age, the more you realise this is you and life isn't long. So get on with it!

Kylie Minogue, b. 1968
Australian singer and actor

The important thing is not what they think of me, it is what I think of them.

Queen Victoria, 1819-1901
British Monarch and Empress of India

Self-discipline

Some people regard discipline as a chore. For me, it is a kind of order that sets me free to fly.

Julie Andrews, b. 1934
British singer and actress

People who are unable to motivate themselves must be content with mediocrity, no matter how impressive their other talents.

Andrew Carnegie, 1835-1919
Scottish/American industrialist and philanthropist

Self-improvement

I know of no more encouraging fact than the unquestioned ability of a man to elevate his life by conscious endeavour.

Henry David Thoreau, 1817-1862
American essayist, poet and mystic

There's only one corner of the universe you can be certain of improving, and that's your own self.

Aldous Huxley, 1894-1963
English writer

Every man has to seek in his own way to make his own self more noble and to realise his own true worth.

Albert Schweitzer, 1875-1965
French medical missionary

I tell you that as long as I can conceive something better than myself I cannot be easy unless I am striving to bring it into existence or clearing the way for it.

George Bernard Shaw, 1856-1950
Irish dramatist, writer and critic

Self-knowledge

Your vision will become clear only when you can look into your heart. Who looks outside, dreams. Who looks inside, awakes.

Carl Jung, 1875-1961
Swiss psychiatrist

Your goal is to find out who you are.

A Course in Miracles

Reason is your light and your beacon of Truth. Reason is the source of Life. God has given you Knowledge, so that by its light you may not only worship him, but also see yourself in your weakness and strength.

Kahlil Gibran, 1883-1931
Lebanese poet, artist and mystic

Who in the world am I? Ah, that's the puzzle.

Lewis Carroll, 1832-1898
English mathematician and author

Resolve to be thyself; and know that he
Who finds himself, loses his misery.

Matthew Arnold, 1822-1888
British writer

To know oneself one should assert himself.

Albert Camus, 1913-1960
Algerian-born French writer

Self-respect

If you put a small value upon yourself you
can be sure that the world will not raise
your price.

Anonymous

Great God, I ask thee for no meaner pelf
Than that I may not disappoint myself.

Henry David Thoreau, 1817-1862
American essayist, poet and philosopher

To have the sense of one's own intrinsic worth, which constitutes self-respect, is potentially to have everything: the ability to discriminate, to love and to remain indifferent. To lack it is to be locked within oneself, paradoxically incapable of either love or indifference.

Joan Didion, b. 1935
American author and journalist

And above all things, never think that you're not good enough yourself. A man should never think that. My belief is that in life people will take you at your own reckoning.

Anthony Trollope, 1815-1882
British novelist

I have to live with myself, and so
I want to be fit for myself to know,
I want to be able as days go by,
Always to look myself straight in the eye.

Edgar A. Guest, 1881-1959
English-born American journalist, poet and author

Simplicity

Remember that very little is needed to
make a happy life.

Marcus Aurelius, 121-180 AD
Roman emperor and philosopher

A truly great man never puts away the
simplicity of a child.

Chinese proverb

The ability to simplify means to eliminate the
unnecessary so that the necessary may speak.

Hans Hofmann, 1880-1966
German-born American painter

Our life is frittered away by detail . . .
Simplify, simplify.

Henry David Thoreau, 1817-1862
American essayist, poet and mystic

Possessions, outward success, publicity, luxury
— to me these have always been contemptible.
I assume that a simple and unassuming manner
of life is best for everyone, best for both the
body and the mind.

Albert Einstein, 1879-1955
German-born physicist

Sisters

Sisters stand between one and life's
circumstances.

Nancy Mitford, 1904-1973
English writer

Sisters, when they do get on, can be closer than
anyone else; closer than parents who are apt to
leave the stage halfway through the play, closer
than husbands or lovers who never knew Act
One. Friends can change and brothers marry.
Sisters tend to stick around.

Jane Gardam, b. 1928
English novelist

I have lost such a treasure, such a sister, such a friend as never can have been surpassed. She was the sun of my life, the gilder of every pleasure, the soother of every sorrow. I had not a thought concealed from her; and it is as if I had lost a part of myself.

Cassandra Austen
From a letter written on the death of her sister, novelist Jane Austen, in 1817

For there is no friend like a sister
In calm and stormy weather;
To cheer one on the tedious way,
To fetch one if one goes astray,
To lift one if one totters down,
To strengthen while one stands.

Christina Rossetti, 1830-1894
English poet

Solitude

Loneliness is the poverty of self; solitude is the richness of self.

May Sarton, 1912-1995
American writer and poet

I was never less alone than when by myself.

Edward Gibbon, 1737-1794
English historian and politician

In solitude we give passionate attention to our lives, to our memories, to the details around us.

Virginia Woolf, 1882-1941
English novelist

Arranging a bowl of flowers in the morning can give a sense of quiet in a crowded day — like writing a poem or saying a prayer. What matters is that one be for a time inwardly attentive.

Anne Morrow Lindbergh, b. 1906
American writer

The best thinking has been done in solitude.
The worst has been done in turmoil.

Thomas Edison, 1847-1931
American inventor

The more powerful and original a mind, the
more it will incline to the religion of solitude.

Aldous Huxley, 1894-1963
English writer

Sorrow

The deeper the sorrow that carves into your
being, the more joy you can contain. Joy and
sorrow are inseparable.

Kahlil Gibran, 1883-1931
Lebanese poet, artist and mystic

Sorrows are our best educators. A man
can see further through a tear than through
a telescope.

Anonymous

Happiness is beneficial for the body, but it is grief that develops the powers of the mind.

Marcel Proust, 1871-1922
French writer

Where there is sorrow there is holy ground.

Oscar Wilde, 1854-1900
Irish dramatist, novelist and wit

The groundwork of life is sorrow. But that once established one can start to build. And until that is established one can build nothing: no life of any sort.

D. H. Lawrence, 1855-1930
British writer, poet and critic

Have courage for the greatest sorrows of life and patience for the small ones, and when you have laboriously accomplished your daily tasks, go to sleep in peace. God is awake.

Victor Hugo, 1802-1885
French poet and writer

Strength

If we are strong, our strength will
speak for itself.
If we are weak, words will be no help.

John F. Kennedy, 1917-1963
President of the United States of America

Our strength lies, not alone in our proving
grounds and our stockpiles, but in our ideals,
our goals and their universal appeal to all men
who are struggling to breathe free.

Adlai Stevenson, 1900-1965
*American statesman, lawyer and United Nations
representative*

Decision is one of the duties of strength.

H. G. Wells, 1866-1946
English writer

Success

Success is all about the quiet accumulation
of small triumphs.

J. P. Donleavy, b. 1926
Irish-born American writer and dramatist

There are two kinds of success. One is the very
rare kind that comes to the man who has the
power to do what no one else has the power to
do. That is genius. But the average man who
wins what we call success is not a genius. He is
a man who has merely the ordinary qualities
that he shares with his fellows, but who has
developed those ordinary qualities to a more
than ordinary degree.

Theodore Roosevelt, 1858-1919
President of the United States of America

We are prone to judge success by the index of
our salaries or the size of our automobiles,
rather than by the quality of our service and
our relationship to humanity.

Martin Luther King, Jr, 1929-1968
American civil rights leader and minister

A minute's success pays the failure of years.

Robert Browning, 1812-1889
English poet

I hope I have convinced you — the only
thing that separates successful people from
the ones who aren't is the willingness to work
very, very hard.

Helen Gurley Brown, b. 1922
American publisher and author

Success is not about money and power. Real
success is about relationships. There's no point
in making $50 million a year if your teenager
thinks you're a jerk and you spend no time
with your wife.

Christopher Reeve, b. 1952
American screen actor

The secret of success is constance to purpose.

Benjamin Disraeli, 1804-1881
British Prime Minister and writer

Self-trust is the first secret of success.

Ralph Waldo Emerson, 1803-1882
American essayist, poet and philosopher

Eighty percent of success is showing up.

Woody Allen, b. 1935
American film director, writer and comedian

The difference between failure and success is doing a thing nearly right and doing a thing exactly right.

Anonymous

My formula for success? Rise early, work late, strike oil.

John Paul Getty, 1892-1976
American oil magnate

The men I have seen succeed have always been cheerful and hopeful, who went about their business with a smile on their faces, and took all the changes and chances to this mortal life like men.

Charles Kingsley, 1819-1875
English writer, poet and clergyman

Success is a state of mind. If you want success, start thinking of yourself as a success.

Anonymous

You must never conclude, even though everything goes wrong, that you cannot succeed. Even at the worst there is a way out, a hidden secret that can turn failure into success and despair into happiness. No situation is so dark that there is not a ray of light.

Norman Vincent Peale, 1898-1993
American writer and minister

Half the things that people do not succeed in, are through the fear of making the attempt.

James Northcote, 1746-1831
English painter

The secret of success is to do the common things uncommonly well.

John D. Rockefeller, 1839-1937
American oil magnate and philanthropist

To succeed in the world we must do all we can to appear successful.

Duc de La Rochefoucauld, 1613-1680
French writer

One only gets to the top rung on the ladder by steadily climbing up one at a time, and suddenly all sorts of powers, all sorts of abilities which you thought never belonged to you — suddenly become within your own possibility and you think, 'Well, I'll have a go, too.'

Margaret Thatcher, b. 1925
British Prime Minister

As is the case in all branches of the arts, success depends in a very large measure upon individual initiative and exertion, and cannot be achieved except by dint of hard work.

Anna Pavlova, 1881-1931
Russian ballet dancer

Do your work with your whole heart and you will succeed — there is so little competition.

Elbert Hubbard, 1856-1915
American writer

There are many paths to the top of the mountain, but the view is always the same.

Chinese proverb

It's Up To You!

If you think you're a winner you'll win.
If you dare to step out you'll succeed.
Believe in your heart, have a purpose to
    start.
Aim to help fellow man in his need.
Thoughts of faith must replace every doubt.
Words of courage and you cannot fail.
If you stumble and fall, rise and stand ten
    feet tall,
You determine the course that you sail.

Anonymous

Suffering

A man who fears suffering is already suffering
from what he fears.

Michel de Montaigne, 1533-1592
French essayist and moralist

Recognising the necessity for suffering I have
tried to make of it a virtue. If only to save
myself from bitterness, I have attempted to see
my personal ordeals as an opportunity to trans-
form myself and heal the people involved in
the tragic situation which now obtains. I have
lived these past few years with the conviction
that unearned suffering is redemptive.

Martin Luther King, Jr, 1929-1968
American civil rights leader and minister

Although the world is very full of suffering, it
is also full of the overcoming of it.

Helen Keller, 1880-1968
Blind and deaf American writer and scholar

Never to suffer would have been never to have been blessed.

Edgar Allan Poe, 1809-1849
American poet and writer

Strength is born in the deep silence of long-suffering hearts; not amid joy.

Felicia Hemans, 1793-1835
British poet

Who will tell whether one happy moment of love, or the joy of breathing or walking on a bright morning and smelling the fresh air, is not worth all the suffering and effort which life implies?

Erich Fromm, 1900-1980
American psychoanalyst

Sympathy

Sympathy is the golden key that unlocks the
hearts of others.

Anonymous

Pity may represent no more than the
impersonal concern which prompts the
mailing of a cheque, but true sympathy is
the personal concern which demands the
giving of one's soul.

Martin Luther King, Jr, 1929-1968
American civil rights leader and minister

Sympathy is thinking with your heart.

Anonymous

T

Tact

Silence is not always tact, and it is tact that is golden, not silence.

Samuel Butler, 1835-1902
English writer

Tact is the ability to describe others as they see themselves.

Abraham Lincoln, 1809-1865
American statesman and President

In the battle of existence, talent is the punch; tact is the clever footwork.

Wilson Mizner, 1876-1933
American writer, wit and dramatist

Thought

Few people think more than two or three times a year. I have made an international reputation for myself by thinking once or twice a week.

George Bernard Shaw, 1856-1950
Irish dramatist, writer and critic

Great thoughts come from the heart.

Marquis de Vauvenargues, 1715-1747
French soldier and writer

As soon as man does not take his existence for granted, but beholds it as something unfathomably mysterious, thought begins.

Albert Schweitzer, 1875-1965
French medical missionary

All that we are is the result of what we have thought; it is founded on our thoughts, it is made up of our thoughts. If a man speaks or acts with a pure thought, happiness follows him, like a shadow that never leaves him.

Buddha, 563-483 BC
Indian religious teacher and founder of Buddhism

Thinking is the talking of the soul with itself.

Plato, c. 429-347 BC
Greek philosopher

It is not best that we should all think alike; it is difference of opinion which makes horse races.

Mark Twain, 1835-1910
American humorist and writer

Time

The moment passed is no longer; the future may never be; the present is all of which man is master.

Jean-Jacques Rousseau, 1712-1778
Swiss-born French philosopher and essayist

Oh, be swift to love! Make haste to be kind. Do not delay; the golden moments fly!

Henry Wadsworth Longfellow, 1807-1882
American poet and writer

A man who dares waste one hour of time has not discovered the value of life.

Charles Darwin, 1809-1882
English naturalist

In reality, killing time
Is only the name for another
of the multifarious ways
By which time kills us.

Sir Osbert Sitwell, 1892-1969
English poet and writer

Enjoy the present hour,
Be thankful for the past,
And neither fear nor wish
Th' approaches of the last.

Abraham Cowley, 1618-1667
English poet and dramatist

Tolerance

All human beings are born free and equal
in dignity and rights.

Universal Declaration of Human Rights

Understanding everything makes one
very tolerant.

Mme Anne de Staël, 1766-1817
Swiss-born French writer

If you cannot mould yourself as you would
wish, how can you expect other people to be
entirely to your liking?

Thomas à Kempis, c. 1380-1471
German monk

No man can justly censure or condemn
another, indeed no man truly knows another.

Sir Thomas Browne, 1605-1682
English physician and writer

You have no idea of the tremendous release and deep peace that comes from meeting yourself and your brothers totally without judgement.

A Course in Miracles

We must respect the other fellow's religion, but only in the sense and to the extent that we respect his theory that his wife is beautiful and his children smart.

H. L Mencken, 1880-1956
American writer, critic and satirist

O God, help us not to despise or oppose what we do not understand.

William Penn, 1644-1718
English Quaker and founder of Pennsylvania

One ought to examine himself for a very long time before thinking of condemning others.

Molière, 1622-1673
French dramatist and actor

Travel

Travelling and freedom are perfect
partners and offer an opportunity to grow
in new dimensions.

Donna Goldfein, b. 1933
American writer

Keep things on your trip in perspective, and
you'll be amazed at the perspective you gain on
things back home while you're away . . . One's
little world is put into perspective by the
bigger world out there.

Gail Rubin Bereny, b. 1942
American writer

Give me the clear blue sky over my head, and
the green turf beneath my feet, a winding road
before me, and a three hours' march to dinner.

William Hazlitt, 1778-1830
British essayist

The wise man travels to discover himself.

James Russell Lowell, 1819-1891
American poet and diplomat

For my part, I travel not to go anywhere, but to go. I travel for travel's sake. The great affair is to move.

Robert Louis Stevenson, 1850-1894
Scottish writer and poet

A traveller. I love his title. A traveller is to be reverenced as such. His profession is the best symbol of our life. Going from — toward; it is the history of every one of us.

Henry David Thoreau, 1817-1862
American essayist, poet and mystic

One of the pleasantest things in the world is going on a journey; but I like to go by myself.

William Hazlitt, 1778-1830
British essayist

Truth

Truth never damages a cause that is just.

Gandhi, 1869-1948
Indian political leader

The pursuit of truth shall set you free — even
if you never catch up with it.

Clarence Darrow, 1857-1938
American lawyer, writer and reformer

Half the misery in the world comes of want of
courage to speak and to hear the truth plainly,
and in a spirit of love.

Harriet Beecher Stowe, 1811-1896
American author and social reformer

Ethical axioms are found and tested not very
differently from the axioms of science. Truth is
what stands the test of experience.

Albert Einstein, 1879-1955
German-born American physicist

The best test of truth is the power of the thought to get itself accepted in the competition of the market.

Oliver Wendell Holmes, 1809-1894
American writer and physician

If you tell the truth you don't have to remember anything.

Mark Twain, 1835-1910
American humorist and writer

I never give them hell. I just tell the truth and they think it's hell.

Harry S. Truman, 1884-1972
American statesman and President

God offers to every mind its choice between truth and repose.

Ralph Waldo Emerson, 1803-1882
American essayist, poet and philosopher

There are no new truths, but only truths
that have been recognised by those who have
perceived them without noticing.

Mary McCarthy, 1912-1989
American writer

It is the calling of great men, not so much to
preach new truths, as to rescue from oblivion
those old truths which it is our wisdom to
remember and our weakness to forget.

Sydney Smith, 1771-1845
English essayist, clergyman and wit

U

Understanding

Everything that I understand, I understand only because I love.

Leo Tolstoy, 1828-1910
Russian writer

I have striven not to laugh at human actions, not to weep at them, nor to hate them, but to understand them.

Benedict Spinoza, 1632-1677
Dutch philosopher

Unity

United we stand, divided we fall.

English proverb

V

Victory

Victory — a matter of staying power.

Elbert Hubbard, 1856-1915
American writer

Victory at all costs, victory in spite of terror,
victory no matter how long and hard the
road may be; for without victory there is
no survival.

Winston Churchill, 1874-1965
British statesman and Prime Minister

In war there is no substitute for victory.

General Douglas MacArthur, 1880-1964
American military leader

Virtue

A virtue to be serviceable must, like gold, be alloyed with some commoner but more durable metal.

Samuel Butler, 1835-1902
English writer

Virtue is its own reward.

John Dryden, 1631-1700
English poet, satirist and dramatist

No one gossips about other people's secret virtues.

Bertrand Russell, 1872-1970
English philosopher, mathematician and writer

Virtue, perhaps, is nothing more than politeness of the soul.

Honoré de Balzac, 1799-1850
French writer

Vocation

Each honest calling, each walk of life, has
its own elite, its own aristocracy based upon
excellence of performance.

James Bryant Conant
Writer

Every calling is great when greatly pursued.

Oliver Wendell Holmes, 1809-1894
American writer and physician

It is well for a man to respect his own
vocation whatever it is and to think himself
bound to uphold it and to claim for it the
respect it deserves.

Charles Dickens, 1812-1870
English writer

Walking

Walking is man's best medicine.

Hippocrates, c. 460-c. 377 BC
Greek physician

Walking not only strengthens the muscles and bones and is good for the heart and digestion, it also relaxes the mind and soothes the spirit. And it doesn't cost a thing. All you need is a pair of comfortable shoes (essential) and a dog (optional). So what are you waiting for? Take at least three long walks a week, and you'll soon be hooked.

Anonymous

Walking is the best possible exercise. Habituate yourself to walk very far.

Thomas Jefferson, 1743-1826
President of the United States of America

Wealth

Riches are for spending.

Francis Bacon, 1561-1626
British philosopher, essayist and courtier

I've been rich and I've been poor;
rich is better.

Sophie Tucker, 1884-1966
American singer

Few rich men own their own property. The
property owns them.

Robert G. Ingersoll, 1833-1899
American lawyer, orator and writer

Increase of material comforts, it may be
generally laid down, does not in any way
whatsoever conduce to moral growth.

Gandhi, 1869-1948
Indian political leader

Unto whomsoever much is given, of him shall
be much required.

St Luke 12:48

Money can't buy happiness, but it
can buy freedom.

Anonymous

Riches are chiefly good because they
give us time.

Charles Lamb, 1775-1834
English essayist

Wealth may be an excellent thing, for it means
power, it means leisure, it means liberty.

James Russell Lowell, 1819-1891
American poet and diplomat

One can never really be too thin or too rich.

Wallis Simpson, Duchess of Windsor, 1896-1986
American socialite and wife of the Duke of Windsor

Riches do not consist in the possession of
treasures but in the use of them.

Napoleon Bonaparte, 1769-1821
French emperor and general

Life's greatest riches have nothing to
do with money.

Anonymous

The day, water, sun, moon, night — I do not
have to purchase these things with money.

Titus Maccius Plautus, c. 254-184 BC
Roman dramatist

Wisdom

Wisdom is to live in the present, plan for the
future and profit from the past.

Anonymous

Wisdom is the right use of knowledge. To know
is not to be wise. Many men know a great deal,
and are all the greater fools for it. There is no
fool so great as the knowing fool. But to know
how to use knowledge is to have wisdom.

Charles Haddon Spurgeon, 1834-1892
British Baptist preacher

Blessed is the man who finds wisdom,
the man who gains understanding, for he
is more profitable than silver and yields
better returns than gold.

Proverbs 3:13-15

Keep me away from the wisdom which
does not cry, the philosophy which does
not laugh and the greatness which does
not bow before children.

Kahlil Gibran, 1883-1931
Lebanese poet, artist and mystic

By three methods may we learn wisdom: first,
by reflection, which is noblest; second, by
imitation, which is easiest; and third,
by experience, which is the bitterest.

Confucius, c.550-478 BC
Chinese philosopher

The growth of wisdom may be gauged exactly
by the diminution of ill-temper.

Friedrich Nietzsche, 1844-1900
German philosopher

The most manifest sign of wisdom is a
continual cheerfulness; a state like that
in the regions above the moon, always
clear and calm.

Michel de Montaigne, 1533-1592
French essayist

Wonder

For a man who cannot wonder is but a pair of spectacles behind which there are no eyes.

Thomas Carlyle, 1795-1881
Scottish historian, essayist and critic

If I had influence with the good fairy who is supposed to preside over the christening of all children, I should ask that her gift to each child in the world be a sense of wonder so indestructible that it would last throughout life.

Rachel Carson, 1907-1964
American writer and biologist

Tyger! Tyger! burning bright
In the forests of the night,
What immortal hand or eye
Could frame thy fearful symmetry?

William Blake, 1757-1827
English poet and artist

The world will never starve for want of
wonders; but only for want of wonder.

G.K. Chesterton, 1874-1936
English writer, poet and critic

It is a wholesome and necessary thing for
us to turn again to the earth and in the
contemplation of her beauties to know the
sense of wonder and humility.

Rachel Carson, 1907-1964
American writer and biologist

I am so absorbed in the wonder of earth and
the life upon it that I cannot think of heaven
and the angels. I have enough for this life.

Pearl S. Buck, 1892-1972
American writer and missionary

Work

Thank God — every morning when you get up — that you have something to do which must be done, whether you like it or not. Being forced to work, and forced to do your best, will breed in you a hundred virtues which the idle will never know.

Charles Kingsley, 1819-1875
English writer, poet and clergyman

Who said you should be happy? Do your work.

Colette, 1873-1954
French writer

Each morning sees some task begun,
Each evening sees its close.
Something attempted, something done,
Has earned a night's repose.

Henry Wadsworth Longfellow, 1807-1882
American poet and writer

Laziness may appear attractive, but work gives satisfaction.

Anne Frank, 1929-1945
Dutch schoolgirl diarist and victim of the Nazis

Work saves us from three great evils: boredom, vice and need.

Voltaire, 1694-1778
French writer, poet and philosopher

If you can't get the job you want, accept any work you can get and do your very best. You could be surprised where it leads.

Anonymous

What is the use of health, or of life, if not to do some work therewith?

Thomas Carlyle, 1795-1881
Scottish historian, essayist and critic

Work is much more fun than fun.

Noel Coward, 1899-1973
English dramatist, actor and composer

My grandfather once told me there were two kinds of people: those who do the work and those who take the credit. He told me to try to be in the first group — there was much less competition.

Indira Gandhi, 1917-1984
Prime Minister of India

Hire yourself out to work that is beneath you rather than become dependent on others.

The Talmud

I long to accomplish a great and noble task, but it is my chief duty to accomplish small tasks as if they were great tasks.

Helen Keller, 1850-1968
Blind, deaf American writer and scholar

Career is too pompous a word. It was a job, and I have always felt privileged to be paid for what I love doing.

Barbara Stanwyck, 1907-1990
American screen actress

There is no point in work unless it absorbs you like an absorbing game. It if doesn't absorb you, if it's never any fun, don't do it.

D. H. Lawrence, 1885-1930
British writer, poet and critic

My father taught me to work, but not to love it. I never did like to work, and I don't deny it. I'd rather read, tell stories, crack jokes, talk, laugh — anything but work.

Abraham Lincoln, 1809-1865
American statesman and President

Work is the grand cure of all the maladies and miseries that ever beset mankind.

Thomas Carlyle, 1795-1881
Scottish historian and essayist

Without work all life goes rotten.

Albert Camus, 1913-1960
Algerian-born French writer

No man needs sympathy because he has to work . . . Far and away the best prize that life offers is the chance to work hard at work worth doing.

Theodore Roosevelt, 1858-1919
President of the United States of America

Worry

What's the use of worrying?
It never was worthwhile,
So, pack up your troubles in your old kit-bag,
And smile, smile, smile.

George Asaf, 1880-1951
American songwriter

The reason why worry kills more people than work is that more people worry than work.

Robert Frost, 1874-1963
American poet

When I look back on all these worries I remember the story of the old man who said on his deathbed that he had had a lot of trouble in his life, most of which never happened.

Winston Churchill, 1874-1965
British statesman and Prime Minister

There are no troubles in my life except the troubles inseparable from being a spirit living in the flesh.

George Santayana, 1863-1952
Spanish philosopher and writer

Worth

A man passes for what he is worth. What he is engraves itself on his face in letters of light.

Ralph Waldo Emerson, 1803-1882
American essayist, poet and philosopher

Y

Yesterday, Today & Tomorrow

Today is yesterday's pupil.

Thomas Fuller, 1608-1661
English clergyman and writer

I've shut the door on yesterday
And thrown the key away —
Tomorrow has no fears for me,
Since I have found today.

Vivian Y. Laramore
American poet

Light tomorrow with today.

Elizabeth Barrett Browning, 1806-1861
English poet

Finish every day and be done with it. You have done what you could. Some blunders and absurdities no doubt crept in; forget them as soon as you can. Tomorrow is a new day; begin it well and serenely and with too high a spirit to be cumbered with your old nonsense. This day is all that is good and fair. It is too dear, with its hopes and invitations, to waste a moment on yesterdays.

Ralph Waldo Emerson, 1803-1882
American essayist, poet and philosopher

Yesterday is a cancelled cheque.
Tomorrow is a promissory note.
Today is ready cash. Use it!

Anonymous

Out of Eternity the new Day is born;
Into Eternity at night will return.

Thomas Carlyle, 1795-1851
Scottish historian, essayist and critic

Do not ask what tomorrow may bring, and count as profit every day that Fate allows.

Horace 65-8 BC
Roman poet

Write in your heart that every day is the best day of the year.

Ralph Waldo Emerson, 1803-1882
American essayist, poet and philosopher

Redeem thy misspent time that's past;
Live this day as if 'twere thy last.

Thomas Ken, 1637-1711
English bishop

As yesterday is history and tomorrow may never come, I have resolved from this day on, I will do all the business I can honestly, have all the fun I can reasonably, do all the good I can do willingly, and save my digestion by thinking pleasantly.

Robert Louis Stevenson, 1850-1894
Scottish writer and poet

Tomorrow is the most important thing in life. Comes into us at midnight very clean. It's perfect when it arrives and it puts itself in our hands. It hopes we've learned something from yesterday.

John Wayne, 1907-1979
American screen actor

The only limit to our realisation of tomorrow will be our doubts of today. Let us move forward with strong and active faith.

Franklin D. Roosevelt, 1882-1945
President of the United States of America

You

Start treating yourself as if you are the most important asset you'll ever have. After all, aren't you?

Anonymous

Be yourself. Nobody is better qualified.

Anonymous

Our problem is that we make the mistake of comparing ourselves with other people. You are not inferior or superior to any human being . . . You do not determine your success by comparing yourself to others, rather you determine your success by comparing your accomplishments to your capabilities. You are 'number one' when you do the best you can with what you have, every day.

Zig Siglar
American motivational writer

Youth

Youth is the time to go flashing from one end of the world to the other . . . to try the manners of different nations; to hear the chimes at midnight; to see the sunrise in town and country; to be converted at a revival; to circumnavigate metaphysics; write halting verses; run a mile to see a fire, and wait all day long in the theatre to applaud *Hernani.*

Robert Louis Stevenson, 1850-1894
Scottish writer and poet

Youth is happy because it has the ability to see beauty. Anyone who keeps the ability to see beauty never grows old.

Franz Kafka, 1883-1924
Austrian novelist

On with the dance! Let joy be unconfined;
No sleep till morn when Youth and Pleasure meet
To chase the glowing Hours with flying feet.

Lord Byron, 1788-1821
English poet

In case you're worried about what's going to become of the younger generation, it's going to grow up and start worrying about the younger generation.

Anonymous

It takes a lifetime to become young.

Pablo Picasso, 1881-1973
Spanish artist

The real lost souls don't wear their hair long and play guitars. They have crew cuts, trained minds, sign on for research on biological warfare, and don't give their parents a moment's worry.

J. B. Priestley, 1894-1984
English writer and dramatist

Z

Zeal

Through zeal, knowledge is gained, through lack of zeal, knowledge is lost. Let a man who knows this double path of gain and loss thus place himself that knowledge may grow.

Buddha, 563-483 BC
Indian religious teacher and founder of Buddhism

Subject Index

Ability, 9
Achievement, 10
Action, 11
Adventurousness, 15
Adversity, 16
Advice, 17
Ageing, 20
Ambition, 28
Anger, 29
Animals, 30
Apology, 32
Attitude, 33
Authority, 35

Balance, 36
Beauty, 37
Beginning, 39
Belief, 40
Best, 41
Blessings, 42
Books, 43
Boredom, 48

Challenges, 49
Change, 50
Character, 53
Children & Parents, 55
Choice, 61
Civility, 62
Comforting Words, 64
Communication, 65
Compassion, 67
Conscience, 68
Contentment, 70

Conversation, 71
Courage, 73
Creativity, 78
Criticism, 81
Crying, 82
Curiosity, 83

Death, 85
Depression, 88
Difficulties, 89
Disappointment, 90
Doubt, 91
Dreams, 92

Education, 93
Effort, 96
Empowerment, 97
Encouragement, 99
Enjoyment, 101
Enthusiasm, 102
Epitaphs, 105
Error, 107
Excellence, 108
Excuses, 108
Experience, 109

Failure, 111
Faith, 113
Faults, 117
Fear, 118
Fools & Foolishness, 120
Forgiveness, 122
Freedom, 124
Friendship, 127

Gardens & Gardening, 138
Genius, 141
Gifts, 144
Giving, 145
Goals, 149
Goodness, 153
Greatness, 155
Growth, 157
Guilt, 159

Habit, 160
Happiness, 161
Hate, 167
Health, 169
Heart, 171
Heaven, 173
Helping, 174
Home, 176
Hope, 178
Humour, 180

Ideals & Idealism, 181
Ideas, 183
Imagination, 184
Imperfection, 186
Independence, 186
Individuality & Conformity, 187
Insight, 191
Intuition, 192
Invention, 192

Joy, 193
Judgement, 195
Justice, 196

Kindness, 197
Knowledge, 199

Laughter, 201
Leadership, 204
Leisure, 205
Life, 206
Loneliness, 212
Love, 213
Luck, 218

Marriage, 220
Mind, 224
Miracles, 225
Mistakes, 226
Morality, 227
Music, 227

Nature, 229

Obstacles, 233
Opportunity, 233
Optimism, 235
Originality, 240

Parting, 241
Peace, 242
Perseverance, 244
Pleasure, 247
Potential, 248
Power, 249
Praise, 250
Prayer, 252
Prejudice, 253
Problems, 254

Regret, 257
Relationships, 259
Relaxation, 261
Religion, 261
Responsibility, 263

Restrictions, 264
Right, 265
Risk, 265

Self-acceptance, 267
Self-confidence, 268
Self-discipline, 269
Self-improvement, 269
Self-knowledge, 271
Self-respect, 272
Simplicity, 274
Sisters, 275
Solitude, 277
Sorrow, 278
Strength, 280
Success, 281
Suffering, 287
Sympathy, 289

Tact, 290
Thought, 291
Time, 292
Tolerance, 294
Travel, 296
Truth, 298

Understanding, 301
Unity, 301

Victory, 302
Virtue, 303
Vocation, 304

Walking, 305
Wealth, 306
Wisdom, 309
Wonder, 311
Work, 313
Worry, 317
Worth, 318

Yesterday, Today &
    Tomorrow, 319
You, 323
Youth, 324

Zeal, 326

Index of Sources

A *Course in Miracles*, 35, 271, 295

Acton, Lord, 126

Addison, Joseph, 44, 71, 81, 129, 161, 164, 169, 219, 228

Adler, Alfred, 88

Alcott, Louisa May, 73, 149

Allen, Woody, 283

Andrews, Julie, 269

Antrim, Minna, 110

Arendt, Hannah, 119, 122

Aristotle, 29, 37, 77, 93, 128

Arnold, Matthew, 206, 272

Asaf, George, 317

Ascham, Roger, 250

Aung San Suu Kyi, 60, 73, 119

Aurelius, Marcus, 50, 144, 153, 274

Austen, Cassandra, 276

Austen, Jane, 23

Bacon, Francis, 91, 107, 139, 199, 306

Baez, Joan, 11, 61

Bagwan Shree Rajneesh, 268

Baldwin, James, 253

Ball, Lucille, 235

Balzac, Honoré de, 303

Bardot, Brigitte, 25

Barrie, J. M., 113, 166, 262

Barrymore, Ethel, 102, 157, 201

Beaverbrook, Lord, 167

Beauvoir, Simone de, 125, 177

Beecher, Henry Ward, 155

Behan, Brendan, 220

Berenson, Bernard, 225

Bereny, Gail Rubin, 296

Bergman, Ingrid, 258

Berlin, Irving, 183

Bhagavad Gita, 70

Bible, The, 65, 66, 94, 124, 146, 147, 148, 195, 197, 214, 307, 309

Bierce, Ambrose, 109

Billings, Josh, 59

Blake, William, 149, 223, 231, 311

Bolton, Robert, 184

Bonaparte, Napoleon, 112, 308

Bone, Pamela, 239

Boswell, James, 136

Bourke, Susan, 55

Brontë, Charlotte, 35, 253

Brontë, Emily, 77, 137

Brooks, Maria, 178

Brough, E. K. 65

Brown, Helen Gurley, 282

Browne, Thomas, 67, 195, 294

Browning, Elizabeth Barrett, 144, 223, 319

Browning, Robert, 26, 30, 122, 282

Bruyere, Jean de La, 148

Buddha, 67, 291, 326

Buck, Pearl. S., 108, 236, 312

Bulwer-Lytton, Edward, 104, 171

Buren, Abigail Van, 54

Burke, Edmund, 155, 226

Burns, Robert, 105, 128

Bush, Barbara, 210

Butler, Samuel, 30, 251, 290, 303

Byron, Lord, 163, 231, 324

Caddy, Eileen, 145, 151, 187, 190, 201

Caldwell, Taylor, 93
Camus, Albert, 272, 316
Capacchione, Lucia, 65, 191
Carlyle, Thomas, 14, 46, 117,
  155, 240, 311, 314, 316,
  320
Carnegie, Dale, 129, 183, 269
Carpenter, Liz, 21
Carroll, Lewis, 202, 271
Carson, Rachel, 311, 312
Casals, Pablo, 57
Case, Elizabeth York, 140
Cassavetes, John, 78
Chagall, Marc, 215
Channing, William Ellery, 240
Chase, Mary Ellen, 262
Chekhov, Anton, 267
Chesterfield, Lord, 74, 96, 260
Chesterton, G. K. 48, 116, 312
Churchill, Winston, 120, 142,
  145, 181, 235, 245, 259,
  302, 318
Cicero, 133, 135, 150, 212
Clark, Karen Kaiser, 50
Clinton, Hillary, 158
Colette, 31, 45, 56, 313
Conant, James Bryant, 304
Confucius, 38, 51, 72, 111,
  153, 172, 178, 227, 310
Congreve, William, 227
Connolly, Billy, 149
Connolly, Cyril, 262
Conrad, Joseph, 75, 182
Coolidge, Calvin, 246
Coward, Noel, 314
Cowley, Abraham, 179, 293
Cozzens, James Gould, 18
Curcio, Joan L. 266
Curie, Marie, 232

Darrow, Clarence, 298
Darwin, Charles, 293
Deffand, Marquise de, 39

Devlin, Bernadette, 266
Diamond, Neil, 207
Dickens, Charles, 37, 42, 58,
  82, 216, 304
Didion, Joan, 263, 273
Dietrich, Marlene, 135
Dinesen, Isak, 255
Disraeli, Benjamin, 14, 107,
  109, 141, 235, 282
Dobson, Henry Austin, 133
Donleavy, J. P., 281
Dostoevsky, Feodor, 30, 56,
  194, 203, 216, 230
Dryden, John, 303
Dulles, John Foster, 242

Earhart, Amelia, 74
Edelman, Marian Wright, 51
Edison, Thomas, 58, 75, 192,
  245, 248, 278
Edwards, Tyron, 86
Einstein, Albert, 83, 181, 184,
  185, 204, 225, 226, 262,
  263, 275, 298
Eisenhower, Dwight D., 202
Eliot, George, 31, 92, 132, 162
Emerson, Ralph Waldo, 29, 54,
  66, 102, 104, 129, 134, 137,
  174, 176, 179, 204, 208,
  219, 256, 283, 299, 318,
  320
Euripides, 195

Farmer, Frances, 128
Field, Sally, 267
Fielding, Henry, 193
Fitzgerald, Ella, 103
Fonda, Jane, 222
Foote, Samuel, 94
Ford, Betty, 57
Ford, Henry, 13, 81, 103, 204,
  226, 233
Forster, Deborah, 127

Forster, E. M., 66
Fox, Muriel, 222
Francis de Sales, St, 122
Frank, Anne, 314
Frankenheimer, John, 100
Franklin, Benjamin, 11, 13, 15, 70, 94, 125, 136, 234, 255
Freud, Sigmund, 224
Friedan, Betty, 188
Fromm, Erich, 215, 288
Frost, Robert, 188, 317
Fry, Christopher, 154
Fry, Stephen, 106
Fuller, Thomas, 29, 89, 123, 319

Gandhi, 242, 298, 306
Gandhi, Indira, 315
Gardam, Jane, 275
Gaulle, Charles de, 16
Getty, John Paul, 283
Gibbon, Edward, 46, 277
Gibran, Kahlil, 11, 17, 58, 87, 94, 136, 146, 159, 171, 175, 180, 185, 199, 200, 221, 232, 241, 252, 258 , 261, 271, 310
Gilbert, W. S., 28
Gillilan, Strickland, 46
Giltinam, Carolyn, 138
Gizatis, Loretta, 174
Godden, Rumer, 139
Goethe, Johann von, 14, 50, 99, 117, 133, 165, 176, 204, 212, 246
Goldberg, Whoopi, 198
Goldfein, Donna, 296
Goldsmith, Oliver, 117
Gough, Vincent Van, 69
Gracian, 89
Grenfell, Joyce, 194
Guest, Edgar A., 252, 273
Guitton, Jean, 240

Hamilton, Alexander, 142
Hammarskjold, Dag, 12, 151
Hanson, Michael, 11
Harris, Corra May, 76
Harris, Sydney J., 95
Harrison, Benjamin, 156
Haskins, Henry S., 90
Hawes, Judy, 151
Hawthorne, Nathaniel, 85
Hayes, Helen, 115, 213
Hazlitt, William, 296, 297
Helps, Arthur, 198
Hemens, Felicia, 288
Hemingway, Ernest, 41, 227
Henderson, Sara, 12, 49, 92, 254
Henry, Margaret, 24
Hepburn, Katharine, 21, 257
Herbert, George, 215
Hesse, Herman, 168
Hickson, William Edward, 246
Hippocrates, 305
Hofmann, Hans, 274
Holmes, Oliver Wendell, 11, 129, 191, 299, 304
Horace, 121, 321
Howitt, Mary Bothan, 56
Hoyt, Daniel W., 131
Hubbard, Elbert, 112, 146, 160, 207, 286, 302
Hugo, Victor, 251, 279
Humbolt, Alexander von, 101
Hume, David, 38
Hutchison, Robert, 170
Huxley, Aldous, 141, 165, 228, 270, 278

Ibsen, Henrik, 53, 189
Ingersoll, Robert G., 188, 306

James, William, 34, 35, 160, 248
Jameson, Anna, 210

Jefferson, Thomas, 46, 92, 166, 249, 305
Jerome, Jerome K., 205
Johnson, Samuel, 72, 76, 84, 95, 134, 199, 209, 245, 247
Jong, Erica, 118
Jonson, Ben, 127, 169
Joubert, Joseph, 95, 185
Joyner, Florence Griffith, 114
Julian of Norwich, 147
Jung, Carl, 36, 150, 271

Kafka, Franz, 324
Kanter, Rosabeth Moss, 246
Keats, John, 39
Keller, Helen, 41, 54, 74, 98, 113, 120, 163, 256, 287, 315
Kelly, Virginia, 238
Ken, Thomas, 321
Kennedy, John F., 150, 233, 243, 280
Kennedy, Robert F., 112, 182
Kenny, Sister Elizabeth, 76
Kent, Corita, 104
Kempis, Thomas à, 294
Kettering, Charles F., 192, 254
Keynes, John Maynard, 183
Khayyam, Omar, 247
Kierkegaard, Soren, 217
King, Martin Luther, 76, 80, 115, 123, 126, 167, 196, 215, 281, 287, 289
Kingsley, Charles, 38, 284, 313
Kinnock, Neil, 67
Kipling, Rudyard, 34, 252
Kitzinger, Sheila, 26
Kübler-Ross, Elisabeth, 34, 86, 125, 187, 213
Kuhn, Margaret, 21

Lamb, Charles, 153, 307
Landers, Ann, 17, 167

Lang, Andrew, 24
Langbridge, Frederick, 239
Lao-Tze, 147, 197
Laramore, Vivian Y., 319
Lawrence, D. H., 86, 279, 316
Lawrence, T. E.,189
Lee, Harper, 68, 75
Le Guin, Eleanor, 45
Lessing, Doris, 158
L'Estrange, Sir Roger, 196
LeTendre, Mary Jean, 52
Lewitzky, Bella, 78, 125
Lichtenberg, George, 142
Lincoln, Abraham, 41, 53, 59, 62, 162, 196, 290, 316
Lindbergh, Anne Morrow, 23, 37, 51, 277
Linkletter, Art, 18
Lombroso, Cesar, 143
Longfellow, Henry Wadsworth, 156, 292, 313
Lowell, Amy, 44
Lowell, James Russell, 51, 132, 146, 297, 307
Lucan, 87
Luther, Martin, 147

MacArthur, Douglas, 158, 233, 302
Macarthur, Elizabeth, 64
Macaulay, Lord, 43
MacDonald, George, 205
Mailer, Norman, 157
Malouf, David, 10
Mann, Horace, 174
Mann, Thomas, 157, 184
Mannes, Marya, 27
Mansfield, Katherine, 131, 132, 257
Maupassant, Guy de, 71
Maxwell, Elaine, 97
McCarthy, Mary, 257, 300
Mead, Margaret, 98, 192

Meir, Golda, 82
Mencken, H. L., 295
Meredith, George, 252
Michelangelo, 143
Midler, Bette, 189
Minogue, Kylie, 268
Mill, John Stuart, 109
Milton, John, 43, 153
Mitford, Nancy, 275
Mizner, Wilson, 290
Montague, Lady Mary
  Wortley, 43
Montaigne, Michel de, 47,
  176, 186, 287, 310
Montesquieu, Charles de, 44
Molière, 295
Morita, Akio, 83
Morris, William,177
Morrison, Jim, 35
Mother Teresa of Calcutta,
  217

Nabokov, Vladimir, 85
Nash, Ogden, 267
Navratilova, Martina, 12
Newhart, Bob, 201
Nicholson, Jack, 258
Niclaus, Jack, 10
Nicolson, Harold, 96
Nietzche, Friedrich, 48, 78,
  168, 190, 310
Nin, Anaïs, 73, 264
Nixon, Richard M., 168
Nolte, Dorothy Law, 60
Northcote, James, 284
Norton, Caroline, 55

O'Keefe, Georgia, 207
Orwell, George, 45
Osborn, Alex F., 79

Paine, Thomas, 40, 249
Parker, Theodore, 90

Pavlova, Anna, 285
Payne, J. H., 178
Peale, Norman Vincent, 9, 32,
  40, 237, 284
Peck, M. Scott, 91, 255
Penn, William, 295
Perkins, Kieren, 99
Phaedrus, 224
Phelps, Elizabeth Stuart, 161
Picasso, Pablo, 27, 325
Plato, 292
Plautus, Titus Maccius, 308
Player, Gary, 218
Poe, Edgar Allen, 288
Ponder, Catherine, 98
Pope, Alexander, 32
Porter, Katherine A., 225
Post, Emily, 71
Potter, Beatrix, 22
Prather, Hugh, 15, 265
Priestley, J. B., 325
Proust, Marcel, 279

Queen Victoria, 268
Quincey, Thomas de, 69

Ransome, Arthur, 234
Reagan, Nancy, 16
Reagan, Ronald, 21, 226
Reeve, Christopher, 282
Rice, Helen Steiner, 213
Rochefoucauld, Duc de la, 14,
  164, 191, 285
Rockefeller, John D., 285
Rogers, Will, 81
Roosevelt, Eleanor, 53, 118,
  130, 187, 203, 206, 211
Roosevelt, Franklin D., 124,
  322
Roosevelt, Theodore, 19, 61,
  266, 281, 317
Rossetti, Christina, 173, 276
Rosten, Leo, 209

Rousseau, Jean-Jaques, 292
Rowland, Helen, 177
Ruskin, John, 186
Russell, Bertrand, 138, 162, 166, 205, 217, 303
Russell, Rebecca, 145

Sai, Baba, 13, 50, 116, 149, 169, 170, 175, 209, 214, 263
Saint-Exupery, Antoine de, 163, 172
Samuel, Herbert, 43
Sand, George, 22, 197
Santayana, George, 90, 134, 166, 208, 318
Sarasate, Pablo, 141
Saroyan, William, 112, 207, 260
Sarton, May, 20, 120, 140, 277
Sawyer, Charles, 178
Schopenhauer, Arthur, 264
Schweitzer, Albert, 161, 175, 238, 270, 291
Scott, John, 139
Scott-Maxwell, Florida, 27
Seneca, 18, 72, 97, 175, 206, 249
Shakespeare, William, 33, 66, 69, 217, 234
Shaw, Geoge Bernard, 52, 63, 86, 164, 184, 205, 244, 254, 270, 291
Shelley, Percy Bysshe, 216
Shenstone, William, 152
Siglar, Zig, 323
Simpson, Wallis, 307
Sitwell, Dame Edith, 79
Smith, Elizabeth Oakes, 114
Smith, Logan Pearsall, 43,
Smith, Sydney, 47, 88, 137, 169, 173, 250, 300

Sodowski, Nina, 115
Solzhenitsyn, Alexander, 154
Sophocles, 130, 216
South, Robert, 145
Spock, Benjamin, 57
Spencer, Herbert, 170
Spinoza, Benedict, 243, 301
Spurgeon, Charles Haddon, 244, 309
Staël, Mme Anne de, 68, 294
Stanwyck, Barbara, 315
Stead, Christina, 223
Stephens, James, 83
Sterne, Laurence, 114, 200
Stevenson, Adlai, 105, 122, 200, 280
Stevenson, Robert Louis, 127, 134, 227, 236, 297, 321, 324
St John, Adela Rogers, 193
Stowe, Harriet Beecher, 144, 244, 298
Streisand, Barbra, 208
Swetchine, Anne Sophie, 77

Tagore, Rabindranath, 115, 208
Talmud, The, 148, 222
Tarkington, Booth, 162
Thackeray, William Makepeace, 59, 131, 259
Thatcher, Margaret, 245, 285
The Lord's Prayer, 123
Theresa, St, 113
Thoreau, Henry David, 68, 135, 231, 232, 253, 269, 272, 274, 297
Thurber, James, 24
Tintoretto, 173
Todd, Mike, 33
Tolkien, J. R. R., 15
Tolstoy, Leo, 301
Tourville, Abbé de, 202

Toynbee, Arnold, 39
Trevelyan, George Macauley, 83
Trine, Ralph Waldo, 42, 188, 230
Trollope, Anthony, 273
Trueblood, D. Elton, 140
Truman, Harry S., 156, 299
Tucker, Sophie, 306
Turland, Heather, 10
Tusser, Thomas, 177
Twain, Mark, 20, 25, 30, 36, 59, 60, 88, 110, 117, 121, 155, 193, 194, 220, 265, 292, 299

Universal Declaration of Independence, 294
Updike, John, 228
Ustinov, Peter, 237

Vauvenargues, Marquis de, 19, 250, 291
Virgil, 9
Voltaire, 314
Vonnegut, Kurt, 47

Waller, Edmund, 173

Ward, Henry Beecher, 59
Warton, Edith, 163
Washington, Booker T., 168
Washington, George, 132
Washington, Martha, 33
Wayne, John, 322
Weatherford, Cathy Warner, 95
Wells, H. G., 280
West, Jessamyn, 123
Whitehorn, Katharine, 221
Whitman, Walt, 31, 229
Wilcox, Ella Wheeler, 85, 198, 238
Wilde, Oscar, 130, 279
Wilder, Thornton, 140, 214
Williams, Tennessee, 124
Winchell, Walter, 128
Winfrey, Oprah, 19, 97
Wittgenstein, Ludwig, 121
Woolf, Virginia, 25, 79, 189, 277
Wordsworth, William, 22, 229,
Wright, Orville, 103
Wright, Wilbur, 103

Yeats, W. B., 133, 154
Young, Edward, 116